ACCLAIM FOR

Jesus and the n

Glen Stassen, Fuller Theological Seminary
In a time when the church is being seduced by the concentration of
power and violence, this book gives us the ethic we need to remain
faithful. Almost all the major themes on which John Howard Yoder
later based his classic *Politics of Jesus* are here – in briefer and highly
readable form.

Andy Crouch, *Re:generation Quarterly*
Trocmé brings a ground-breaking historical clarity to Jesus' life and
teachings. The result is a vision for Jesus' followers that is unsettling,
exhilarating, and – most amazing of all – possible.

John Dear, author, *Jesus the Rebel*
Gandhi once said that Jesus was the greatest practitioner of nonviolence
in history and that the only people who do not know that Jesus was
nonviolent are Christians. Now more than ever, we need to study and
imitate the nonviolent Jesus. This classic text by a legendary Christian
peacemaker is a must for anyone who is concerned not only about the
world's wars and violence, but who wants to know what Jesus would
do. It is a great source of inspiration and encouragement.

Donald Kraybill, author, *The Upside-Down Kingdom*
The revised edition is a welcome refinement to a classic study…Trocmé
has the prophetic gift of bypassing doctrinal fluff and cutting to the
heart of Jesus' message: a stark call for repentance, love and socio-economic change. A prophet for the 21st century, Trocmé speaks in plain
and simple words we can understand but may not want to hear. Read
him with caution: this book may change your life.

Ched Myers, author, *Who Will Roll Away the Stone?*
Trocmé pioneered territory where many of us now dwell, and opened
doors we seek still to pass through…It is wonderful that a new generation might come to know this book: it represents a continuing light in
our darkness.

Stanley Hauerwas, Duke Divinity School
This book – and especially this newly expanded edition – deserves to be more widely known…Trocmé's focus saves any account of salvation from pietistic distortion…His comparison of Gandhi and Jesus is also extremely important.

Charles Scriven, author, *The Transformation of Culture*
In this new edition of Trocmé's classic work, the genius of a pastor-revolutionary shines through once more, magnified under the light of notes that reinforce his startling conception of witness and hope.

Craig Keener, Eastern Seminary
Trocmé's courage in the face of Nazi oppression is reason enough to give him a fresh hearing in a world of continuing injustice and rising ethnic hatreds. One need not agree with every point to learn from his vision of justice – a vision to which we often give lip-service while neglecting its challenge in our daily lives.

Richard Cassidy, author, *Paul in Chains*
This volume deserves wider recognition as the classic it truly is. Plough is to be congratulated for this splendid edition.

Craig L. Blomberg, Denver Seminary
In an age of ever-increasing war and terror, Plough has done scholars, pastors and thoughtful laypersons all a great service by editing and reprinting this classic work on the nonviolent way of Jesus. Practicing what he preached, Trocmé helped save many Jews from the Nazis. His work inspired the late John Howard Yoder, and compares favorably with current authors such as Walter Wink and Glen Stassen. Not everyone will agree with every exegetical detail, but all will feel the compelling force of Trocmé's cumulative case. This is a book worth pondering at length.

Walter Wink, Auburn Theological Seminary
Jesus and the Nonviolent Revolution is one of the most important writings on nonviolence ever penned. Trocmé not only lays out his principles with astonishing clarity, but he lived them out at great risk. I can think of no better place to begin the study of this timely subject.

Jesus and the Nonviolent Revolution

Jesus and the Nonviolent Revolution

ANDRÉ TROCMÉ

Edited by Charles E. Moore

PLOUGH PUBLISHING HOUSE

Published by Plough Publishing House
Walden, New York
Robertsbridge, England
Elsmore, Australia
www.plough.com

André Trocmé's book *Jesus and the Nonviolent Revolution* was first published in English in 1973 by Herald Press, Scottdale, PA 15683, translated from the French by Michael H. Shank and Marlin E. Miller. This revised and expanded edition incorporates material from *The Politics of Repentance* by André Trocmé, used by permission of Fellowship Publications, Nyack, NY 10960.

Scripture taken from the *Holy Bible, New International Version.* Copyright © 1973, 1978, 1984 International Bible Society. Used by permission of Zondervan. All rights reserved.

Cover art © Daniel Bonnel, www.ImagesOnChrist.com.

18 17 16 15 14   8 7 6 5 4 3 2 1

ISBN 10: 0-87486-927-7
ISBN 13: 978-0-87486-927-9

A catalog record for this book is available from the British Library.
    Library of Congress Cataloging-in-Publication Data

Trocmé, André, 1901-1971
    [Jésus-Christ et la révolution non violente. English]
    Jesus and the nonviolent revolution / André Trocmé ; edited by
Charles E. Moore.– Rev. and expanded ed.
        p. cm.
Includes bibliographical references and index.
    isbn 0-87486-927-7 (pbk. : alk. paper)
    1. Jesus Christ–Teachings. 2. Nonviolence–Biblical teaching. 3.
Revolutions–Biblical teaching. i. Moore, Charles E., 1956- ii. Title.
    bs2417.p2 t7613 2003
    232.9'54–dc21
                                        2002015610
Printed in the USA

Contents

Introduction

Few books stand the test of time as this one has. Perhaps the fact that it is still so relevant rests in the circumstances of its genesis – in the courageous life of its author. Since it first appeared in English in 1972, André Trocmé's *Jesus and the Nonviolent Revolution* has influenced a whole stream of New Testament thinkers and peace activists. Dozens of books about Christian ethics make reference to it, and proponents of nonviolence turn to it repeatedly for guidance. For example, significant portions of John Howard Yoder's classic *Politics of Jesus* are based on Trocmé's thesis. However, one cannot fully appreciate Trocmé's ideas without some understanding of the man and of the amazing life story that forms the context for his message.

The Story of Le Chambon

André Trocmé was born into a French-German family in 1901, at the dawn of a turbulent period that would eventually catapult all Europe into armed conflict. As a young man, André's youthful enthusiasm and impulsive deeds made him stand out. When the German army was rapidly marching into Northern France, he excitedly hung a French flag from the topmost branches of a towering tree near his house.

During the First World War, André saw first-hand the horrors and senselessness of that war. At the age of thirteen he simply could not accept that his German cousins, his mother being German, might fight against his own half brothers. The shock of this, along with the senseless death of his mother from a car accident just prior to the war, and his encounter with numerous pacifist theologians after the war, cemented his orientation as a pacifist. Moreover, as a young student, he realized that military armistices could not establish peace between nations or reconstruct the moral fabric of a society.

Years later he would be described by one writer as "a man of mystical fervor, aggressively loving, almost explosive in his rush to save lives." But his path was not always so clear. As the specter of National Socialism began to haunt Europe, Trocmé, despite his aversion to violence, conceded that it might be necessary to plot against and assassinate Hitler. In the end he joined an altogether different kind of conspiracy, one that chronicler Philip Hallie called "a conspiracy of goodness."

By the time Hitler's war machine came to full force, Trocmé, now married and a father of four, was co-pastor of the French Reformed Church in Le Chambon sur Lignon. A farming village on a pine-studded plateau in the mountains of south-central France, Le Chambon seemed an unlikely breeding place for the radical resistance for which it would soon be famous. Yet it became a magnet to a stream of refugees that included both French and foreign Jews, providing shelter and safety from their persecutors.[1]

Already before the first Jews arrived, others fleeing from Franco's regime in Spain, and later from the Nazis, found this Protestant sanctuary, consisting of twelve villages, willing to bid them welcome. In the parish of Le Chambon, Trocmé and his fellow pastor, Edouard Theis, united the people in the effort to protect these fugitives, exhorting their parishioners to live not in fear of the state, but according to moral conviction. What eventually became a massive, organized network to protect and even educate Jewish children who had been taken out of internment camps, started at the grassroots with these first refugees. Villagers and farmers opened their homes to the refugees, sometimes to stay, sometimes to wait until accommodations could be arranged elsewhere or until they could be smuggled across the Swiss border. Besides the hospitality of individuals, by the middle of the occupation financial aid from outside the village was supporting seven larger houses of refuge. Several humanitarian organizations helped to established boardinghouses for refugee children as well as a student center.

So it came about that resisting authority became a normal part of daily life in Le Chambon. The students at the private school L'École Nouvelle Cévenole, which Trocmé and Theis had founded, refused to salute the flag or hang the picture of Pétain, the Vichy leader, in every classroom. On a national holiday, Trocmé's parish ignored Pétain's order to ring the church bells at noon. They would ring the bells only for God. A tight network also provided the refugees with false identification cards that allowed them to pass as non-Jewish. But though it was truly resistance, the fighters in this nonviolent underground were not fueled by anger or hatred. Some maintained connections with partisan fighters in the area, while throughout the rescue effort anonymous messages and phone calls trickled in at just the right time warning of the possibility of raids by the Vichy police. Because of the risk of discovery, town residents never talked in public about their deeds.

Trocmé, at considerable personal risk, was at the forefront of much of the village's activity. On June 22, 1940, France surrendered to the Nazis and agreed to arrest and deport to Germany

any refugees Hitler's government might demand. The next day, during a Sunday service, Trocmé and Theis both preached about resistance.

> Tremendous pressure will be put on us to submit passively to a totalitarian ideology. If they do not succeed in subjugating our souls, at least they will want to subjugate our bodies. The duty of Christians is to use the weapons of the Spirit to oppose the violence that they will try to put on our consciences. We appeal to all our brothers in Christ to refuse to cooperate with this violence...
>
> Loving, forgiving, and doing good to our adversaries is our duty. Yet we must do this without giving up, and without being cowardly. We shall resist whenever our adversaries demand of us obedience contrary to the orders of the gospel. We shall do so without fear, but also without pride and without hate.[2]

Their sermon, if daring, was also timely. The Vichy government lost no time in implementing the Nuremberg laws and immediately began arrests. Jews and other refugees were zealously herded into internment camps. But Trocmé, true to his preaching, was not about to admit defeat. With the approval of his church council, and at the request of the American Friends Service Committee, he began to search for ways to provide refuge in Le Chambon for the children rescued from the camps – a dangerous and illegal undertaking. There the recently founded École Nouvelle Cévenole, as well as the public school, stood ready to assimilate them. He also urged his congregation to continue to shelter fugitives of "the people of the Bible," and encouraged them to stay firm.

In the summer of 1942, Minister Georges Lamirand, head of the Vichy government's youth organization, showed up in Le Chambon and delivered a speech on the "New Social Order." The speech over, he was immediately handed a letter by the local youth, protesting the recent roundup of nearly 13,000 Jews in Paris. They informed him in unequivocal terms that they intended to protect persecuted people whenever and however they could. Trocmé was clearly the source of this defiance, and soon after was warned of the dire consequences facing him if he did not turn in the names of all hidden Jews. Trocmé refused, saying, "We do not know what a Jew is; we only know people." For three weeks the police scoured the village and its surrounding areas, but the rescue network was so tight that they came up with only two arrests.

In August, under surveillance and with rumors circulating that he might soon be arrested, Trocmé preached to an overflowing church on Deuteronomy 19, concerning the entitlement of the persecuted to shelter, "so that innocent blood will not be shed." His own response was clear: "These people came here for help and for shelter. I am their shepherd. A shepherd does not forsake his flock."

Eventually, though, Trocmé's activities were brought to a halt. In February of 1943 he and Theis, his co-pastor, as well as the director of Le Chambon's public school, were arrested and shipped to a French internment camp. Surprisingly, after four weeks of imprisonment all three men were freed, even though they refused to sign a declaration of obedience. However, Trocmé and Theis were warned that their lives were in danger, so the two men went into hiding for the next ten months but secretly stayed in contact with rescue efforts. Four months after their arrest, the German police finally raided Les Roches, the center for young adult refugees near Le Chambon. This hit close to home for Trocmé; his cousin Daniel, director of Les Roches, was arrested along with seventeen students. He was later murdered by the Nazis at Maidanek, just weeks before the concentration camp was liberated.

The great war finally played itself out. The fighting ended, and the need for secrecy passed. The people of Le Chambon and of the surrounding plateau had kept thousands of innocent lives from harm right to the end, despite repression and intimidation.

Ultimately, the rescue network provided a haven or safe passage for an estimated 2,500 refugees, with a large percentage being Jews and children.[3] And everything took place right under the noses of the Vichy police and, later, of the Gestapo themselves.

Missionary of Nonviolence

Trocmé, in the words of Marlin Miller, who helped translate this book, "was one of the rare Christian pacifists who refused to choose between impassioned action and intellectual clarity." His efforts, which sprang from his clarity of purpose, would be devoted to peace and reconciliation for the remainder of his life. World War II over, Trocmé served from 1948 to 1960 as European secretary for the Fellowship of Reconciliation, traveling and lecturing all over the world. His House of Reconciliation, an international peace center in Versailles, positioned him as one of the links in a chain that united such leaders of nonviolence as Martin Luther King, Jr., Toyohiko Kagawa, and Gandhi.

Driven by his faith, Trocmé and his wife, Magda, set out in 1956 to study the conflict in war-torn Algeria. For a short while there they volunteered their personal time in overcoming illiteracy. They also learned more about the plight of French resisters who refused to serve in the French army. This concerned Trocmé tremendously. He thus worked with the Mennonites to help found Eirene in Morocco, which has now become a worldwide service program for conscientious objectors and development workers.

In 1960, for what was to be the final decade of his life, Trocmé returned to pastoral ministry. Because of his absolute pacifist stand it was difficult for him to find a French church to lead. Finally, he was invited to become pastor of a large Reformed church in Geneva, Switzerland. Despite the bourgeois lives of his congregants, he motivated them to organize and support technical development work in northern Algeria. Shortly before his death,

Yad Vashem awarded him and his wife, along with others in Le Chambon, the prestigious "Righteous Among the Nations" medal for the part they played in the rescue efforts.

Trocmé's convictions and ideas grew out of his activities as a peacemaker. His writings were forged not in theoretical musings, but in the fiery events that had been his baptism into the world of nonviolent revolution.

Trocmé wrote much and often but only managed to publish two books. His first book, *The Politics of Repentance* (1953), proposed a strategy for peacemaking in situations of conflict. *Jesus and the Nonviolent Revolution* (1961, French edition), is a systematic treatment of Christian nonviolence and the more influential of the two books.

When this book first appeared it broke the clutches of "Christian realism," spearheaded by Reinhold Niebuhr, which was so dominant at the time. Trocmé offers a truly Christ-centered social ethic, one to be taken seriously not just by individuals but by the church. He understands from personal experience that Christ's redemptive work extends far beyond the individual to encompass society and nations. His understanding of discipleship is revolutionary without succumbing to political ideology or sheer activism.[4]

There is nothing fancy about Trocmé's approach. With prophetic intuition rather than weighty analysis, he renders interpretations that are both subtle and provocative. His core argument is simple: Jesus inaugurated the kingdom of God based on the Jubilee principles of the Old Testament. These principles call for a political, economic, and spiritual revolution in response to human need. Jesus intended nothing less that an actual revolution, with debts forgiven, slaves set free, and land returned to the poor.

It was this threat to vested interests that awakened the hostility toward Jesus that led to the cross. Jesus understood the kingdom of God in terms of God's work in human history; every sphere of life was a domain for God's rulership. But he saw, too, that such rulership would always cost a struggle. The first Christians, who were charged with seditiously "turning the world upside down," understood their master well. They had caught this vision and begun to live it out.

Trocmé is careful to locate Jesus within the socio-cultural context of his day. He therefore expends a great deal of effort surveying various movements, social groups, and patterns of authority and influence that situate Jesus and help to delineate his unique mission. Jesus' way transcended the alternatives of his day, while at the same time it grew out of intense interaction with his contemporaries. Jesus was no spiritual mystic. He had to overcome the temptations of employing violence, of escaping into the desert, and of compromise.

Yet, as Trocmé shows, Jesus refused both the way of violence and of spiritual quietism. He called for practical changes but rejected violence as a means of achieving social change. Instead he articulated and exemplified a way of life that obviates the kind of social order that produces injustice and poverty, and the violence inherent in them. Jesus' nonviolence was not a philosophy or a tactic, but a matter of obedience to God.

Trocmé makes it clear that Jesus should be the center of the church's life and practice, not nonviolence or revolution or justice. Jesus' nonviolent revolution, and ours, is rooted in the cross. Jesus was ready to sacrifice his "cause," the liberation of his people, for the sake of a single human being in need of healing. Human need—be it physical, emotional, spiritual, or social—was Jesus' reason for being, and should be ours. Jesus' sacrifice makes possible a new social order where human lives are dignified with justice, uplifted in compassion, and nurtured by peace.

Trocmé takes the liberty of interpreting certain passages of Scripture in fresh ways. Though somewhat imaginative at times, he puts forth insights that in the broader narrative of Jesus' life make perfect sense. Historical and exegetical work have subsequently proven Trocmé, if not right, then at least on the right track. His work is constructive as well. By showing us how Christ continues to do his work here and now through his people, he broadens our understanding of Jesus' mission, and makes plain what Jesus expected of his followers.

By any standard, Trocmé's work deserves ongoing attention. This edition is new in several respects. First, the text has been edited to read more smoothly. Some material has been rearranged with new subtitles, certain sections deleted to eliminate repetition, and transitional phrases added that were not in the original English edition. New material has also been incorporated, particularly in chapters 14 and 15, which are from Trocmé's book, *The Politics of Repentance*. Finally, references have been added to show how trends in current thought affirm Trocmé's thesis.

Not much has changed since World War II, the Holocaust, and the Cold War. Ours is still an age of bloodshed. We live by the hellish logic of revenge, just war, might makes right, and deterrent force, while inequality, oppression, and exploitation flourish. *Jesus and the Nonviolent Revolution* refutes such logic. Trocmé answers our continued propensity toward violence with, as he terms it, "the algebra of God's kingdom." If only more Christians were courageous enough to follow Trocmé's lead in obedience to Jesus' call, the story of Le Chambon sur Lignon would not be so exceptional.

Charles E. Moore

Preface

There is no easy peace. The earth's exploding population renders more difficult each day a peaceful solution to the problems of hunger, national security, and social justice. Simultaneously, the threat of nuclear destruction continues to hover over the future of humanity.

Meanwhile, the gap widens between the mentality of our contemporaries, shaped by a technological civilization whereby we control nature, and traditional religion, conceived during a rural epoch when human beings bowed under the weight of nature. Though technology threatens human existence more than it ever did in times past, Christian thought—frightened by the responsibilities it should assume—refuses to see in the gospel anything but a message of individual salvation. It might even be said that today's Christianity finds suspect any actions performed for the physical salvation of the human race. It spurns any practical efforts of authentic Christian obedience as presumptuous and pharisaical—and that in an age much in need of them. Such a reversal of the teachings of Jesus Christ must be rectified, lest the church disqualify itself as an instrument capable of pointing the way for a humanity bordering on collective suicide.

I am neither a professor of history nor of theology, and the following little more than scratches the surface of areas normally reserved for specialists. Let me say, however, that having flirted with the theologies and philosophies of despair, I have now rejected their poison. Existential thought may sate one with its lucid analyses, which define the problems, but it fails to offer a courageous obedience capable of resolving them. Such an approach is nothing but a subtle excuse to evade one's responsibilities in the world and is thus characteristic of a period of moral and religious decadence. In fact, the tendency of Christians to intellectualize ethical issues is in direct proportion to the extent that they have become a part of the power establishment.

All of us, Christian and non-Christian alike, are responsible for the hunger, injustice, egoism, exploitation, and wars that devastate our time. Christians bear special responsibility: knowing that God can change both people and their situations, the disciple of Jesus can help bring into being God's future for humanity.

Christians profess that at a given place and time, God intervened in history, rendering all subsequent happenings on this planet as of divine importance. Because of the birth, life, death, and resurrection of Jesus Christ, we know that every birth, every life, and every death matters to God.

If each person has thus been invested with such value, how great is the worth of the sum of human history! Whether one believes he is the Son of God or not, Jesus *is* the central event of history, because *de facto* his coming changed humankind. We must therefore understand who this Jesus was in order to fully grasp the value of humanity and of our task toward it.

Recent works have reopened the debate about who Jesus was.[1] Everyone agrees that when the authors of the New Testament attempted to present Jesus to the people of their generation, they made use of certain beliefs then current in the Mediterranean basin. Obviously, Jesus and his disciples spoke the language of their contemporaries. This should not alarm us. We need not, for example, dispute the value of what people of the first century said about the universe simply because our knowledge of the universe has since expanded. Behind the vocabulary of Jesus' day, we can still discover the enduring Christ.

The gospel merits being read not only with faith, but with intelligence. This does not mean we have to give way to the demythologizing zeal of some interpreters, whose efforts to weed out the gospel have only transformed it into a desert.

If the New Testament has to be demythologized at all, it should be done with the assistance of the Old Testament, not our modern myths.[2] The more one adheres to the strict monotheism of the God of Israel, the more visible the thought of Jesus Christ becomes. The God of Jesus Christ is the God of Israel. The Christian faith dissolves into pure mythology as soon as it no longer leans upon Judaism. True, the authors of the New Testament borrowed from sources other than the Old Testament in order to explain Jesus to their Jewish and Greek contemporaries. But let us not forget that their main frame of reference was always the Old Testament.

Conversely, the Old Testament stands in need of the New. Jesus lifts the crushing fact of the original Fall and broadens the dogma of a narrowly elected people. He humanizes the ritual laws of Moses. He accomplishes what the prophets of old could only announce. Thus one loses nothing by Christianizing Judaism, because Jesus Christ has already done so.

The Jesus of history actually transcends both the Old and the New Testament. He is the point of encounter between two theological edifices, the Jewish and the Christian. He has fulfilled the first and engendered the second. He alone explains that which came before and that which came after him. One does not put a lamp under a bowl, but uses it to lighten the darkness. The light dawns when we let Jesus himself interpret Judaism and Christianity for us.

Jesus' life and teaching are a bridge connecting two historical epochs – a bridge defined by the parables and aphorisms which he spoke. We should try to grasp their deeper meaning. Their depth is more striking than any rigorously consistent doctrine, for they spring from the presence in Jesus of the living God, who reveals himself as the loving Father of all people. God's presence manifests itself; it does not prove itself.

I have thus limited my ambitions to the modest goal of interrogating Jesus Christ by Jesus Christ. What have I discovered? In short, the portrait of a vigorous revolutionary capable of saving the world without using violence.

Although I have examined secondary literature, I wish to underline again my limited exegetical and historical competence. My many other activities have simply prohibited me from doing much scholarly work.[3] The theses concerning the proclamation of a biblical Jubilee by Jesus are my own. If their somewhat unusual character can stimulate the curiosity of the specialists and provoke further inquiry into the social ethics and nonviolence of Jesus, I will have attained my goal.

André Trocmé

PART I

Jesus and His Revolution

CHAPTER ONE

Jesus the Jew

In Jesus' time Galilee was a place in transition. Three languages—
Hebrew, Aramaic, and Greek—were used. Dualistic doctrines
from the east on the devil, angels, and demons threatened belief
in strict Jewish monotheism. Hellenistic civilization was invading
the last strongholds of Judaism. Raised in this complex environment,[1] Jesus could have laid the foundations of his movement by
simply borrowing from all the surrounding sources. But he didn't.

We need merely to read the synoptic Gospels[2] to discover that
Jesus was, at the very least, a Jewish prophet, the last in a line that
had begun with Amos and ended with John the Baptist. Matthew
in particular had one obvious intention: to demonstrate that Jesus
was truly the Messiah whom the prophets had announced. Hence
his generous use of Old Testament quotations.

The Gospels in general had no trouble showing the Jewish character of Jesus' thought. And this is for good reason. Jesus, as a Jew,
had only one library at his disposal, namely the Law of Moses, the
Prophets, and the Psalms. These scriptures inspired his teachings
and parables. Jesus' contemporaries made no mistake on this score.
Even the ones who refused to recognize him as the Messiah saw
him as an authentic prophet.[3] The theology and moral teaching

of Jesus was nothing less than Jewish theology and Jewish moral teaching without the ritual elements. "You diligently study the Scriptures…These are the Scriptures that testify about me" (John 5:39). "I have not come to abolish the Law and the Prophets but to fulfill them," he affirmed. "What did Moses command you?" he asked his questioners. When he gave the Golden Rule, "Do to others what you would have them do to you," still considered the supreme lay expression of morality, he justified it with a peculiarly Jewish expression, "for this sums up the Law and the Prophets" (Matt. 7:12).

The Law of Moses, enlarged and commented upon by the prophets, was *the* law of the Jewish people. It mixed together religious, moral, social, and political prescriptions. When the prophets sounded their calls they addressed themselves to Israel – the people of God. They thought of Judah and Jerusalem as corporate personalities. They thus called the entire people of God to repentance. Justice had to be restored, religion purified, customs transformed, and the Torah put into practice at all levels. Similarly, Jesus addressed his reproaches and his appeals to the entire Jewish people. When he proclaimed *metanoia,* that is, a radical change of heart and mind, he was not addressing himself to pagan "nations," per se, but to the Israelite community. Jesus traveled up and down Galilee preaching the good news of the kingdom, the reign of God: "The time has come. The kingdom of God is near. Repent and believe the good news!" (Mark 1:15). When he commissioned the twelve apostles, he instructed them: "Do not go among the Gentiles or enter any town of the Samaritans. Go rather to the lost sheep of Israel" (Matt. 10:5–6).[4]

Keeping in mind that the Jewish faith was a national religion, it is worth noting that Jesus accepted and taught without hesitation several typically Jewish notions. For instance, Jesus' universalism did not spring from Greek rationalism, or from

Roman law, or from some Enlightenment conception of individual rights. It was also certainly not the offspring of a happy marriage between Judaism and Neoplatonism. It grew out of a Judaism that "exploded" under the pressure and dynamism of the messianism borne within it. Greek and Roman ideals were simply too well balanced, too symmetrical to inspire action. Jesus' universalism, rooted as it was in Judaism's understanding of redemptive history was, on the contrary, asymmetrical. It contained a creative impulse that continuously renewed itself. How so? Consider the following.

The Chosen People

The Old Testament recounts how God chose Abraham of Ur. "Leave your country, your people and your father's household and go to the land I will show you. I will make you into a great nation and I will bless you...I will bless those who bless you, and whoever curses you I will curse; and all peoples on earth will be blessed through you" (Gen. 12:1–3). This sense of election, which pious Jews still believe in today, continues to cause suffering for the Jews and to be a scandal for non-Jews. Yet precisely because of its scandalous character and the disequilibrium it inspires, the notion of election generates movement and energy. This helps explain why the Jewish people has survived centuries of persecution intact, while other civilizations have come and gone.

Following in Israel's footsteps, the church also understands itself as divinely chosen. It affirms that there is no salvation apart from Jesus Christ, and it undertakes in his name the conquest of the world through its reforming and charitable missions. This conviction of having been chosen by God has sadly and unnecessarily created tragic tensions between the Christian faith and other religions. Yet every time the church doubts its election, every time it plays down the "scandal of particularity," its capacity to witness to the gospel also diminishes.

Whereas the Western church has lost much of its conquering dynamism, many in the proletariat, or working class, now consider themselves heirs of Christianity's chosenness. Perhaps because they are "free from the sin of exploitation," the poor have increasingly felt called to guide humanity in the "movement of history." The oppressed thus compel the Christian West to arouse itself from the rationalistic torpor that it so much enjoys.[5]

But let us return to Israel's election. It is the result of a divine choice as inexplicable as love, because Israel is "the least of the nations." Strangely enough, even though God's choice is arbitrary, it binds the responsibility of the elect. For if God makes a covenant with Israel to which he will be faithful, Israel is in return required to uphold its part of the agreement. Israel must be "holy," or "set apart," because it is to be a witness among the nations, with God as its light. As a result of this witness, all nations will eventually recognize that Israel's God is the only one worthy of worship. But if Israel breaks the stipulations of the covenant and becomes unfaithful to Yahweh, terrible punishments will come. God's people will be devastated, carried off in bondage, and destroyed. Only a small remnant will escape. And with this remnant God will again rebuild a faithful people.[6]

Jesus obviously shared this belief in Israel's election. Precisely because of his Jewishness he addresses his prophetic call to the people of Israel. And having drawn the consequences of the Jews' disobedience, he dared to announce the rejection of this stiff-necked people, while also envisioning the birth of a "remnant," of a "small flock," to which the Father would give the kingdom and to which the nations would be drawn.[7]

The Moral Bias

Perhaps even more important than the belief in election is Israel's moral sense, or what we shall call the "moral bias of the Old

Testament." Like the Greek philosophies, Oriental cosmogonies try to explain the creation of the world and the origin of evil and death. Yet humanity always comes out as the victim of fate. Some refer to the Fall as a cosmic catastrophe; others explain evil as the necessary shadow cast by the good. For some, creation is subjected to the perpetual cycle of death and new beginnings. For others, the problem of evil is resolved by successive reincarnations of the human soul until its final absorption into God. The majority find consolation for the world's injustices in the hope for a celestial paradise where sin and death will be abolished.[8]

The Old Testament, on the other hand, dares to attribute evil and death to a strictly moral cause. Death enters history because of humanity's fault. And it is man who drags the other creatures with him into death.[9] At first glance, such notions seem revolting. How can Genesis be reconciled with modern paleontology and evolutionary views that tell us that disease and death affected plants and animals long before man ever appeared on earth? Moreover, if the Old Testament is right, the righteous should be rewarded for their virtues. But how many depraved families enjoy impudent happiness, and how many virtuous ones are struck by inexplicable catastrophes! How many inoffensive nations are annihilated while the brute force of unscrupulous conquerors prevails! No. Humanity's sin cannot be the only cause of suffering and death. Job and the Old Testament psalmists already protested against such an unjust doctrine.

However, there is another way, asymmetric to be sure, of looking at the biblical notion of the Fall and its consequences. It demands that we abandon the search for an *explanation* of evil and death. When we look deeper into the Bible we discover something very different, something that incites action. Here I am, thrown into the world, a person alone before the God of Israel. I cannot declare, "I was born by chance," or "I am conditioned by my environment, the toy of heredity and of events that drag me along." No, I must allow myself to be "offended."[10] What? God says *I* am the only one to blame for my sins? Yes. The only master of my temperament? Yes! Of my environment? Certainly. Of my nation and the way it behaves? Indeed. Of my death and the fall of a world headed straight for suicide? Exactly. The Bible describes how we are all responsible for our death and the death of those around us. And because the Bible is not a philosophical dissertation, it adds one paradox to another by stating that we are guilty because we reject forgiveness. We would not be guilty if our heredity had no cure, but we are guilty insofar as we neglect the cure that God freely gives us.

Jesus gave no other explanation to those who questioned him about the death of eighteen people crushed by a falling tower. "Do you think that they were more guilty than all the others living in Jerusalem? I tell you, no! But unless you repent, you too will all perish" (Luke 13:4). In other words, repentance comes first. Fall on your knees before God and confess your sin. Then get up and change the course of history!

In the Hebrew world, there is no explanation of evil. Redemptive history shows us a different way to get out of it: repentance and faith. By requiring us to repent, God acts in history not so much as Creator, but as Redeemer. Through the repentance of a few, God says to the whole of a sick history, "Rise and walk!" Such an injunction awakens in every person who hears it the response of faith. Such faith gives humanity its true measure and moves history forward. This is the gospel of the kingdom of God.

Inexorable Justice

The asymmetrical nature of Hebrew thought, and thus of Jesus' approach, can also be found in its requirement of justice. Take, for example, the law of retaliation expressed for the first time in the Book of Genesis after Cain had killed his brother. Abel's blood demanded revenge. Justice had to be established. Cain was to die because he had killed. But God decreed that whoever would kill Cain must also pay the price of blood: "If anyone kills Cain, he will suffer vengeance seven times over." "Whoever sheds the blood of man, by man shall his blood be shed; for in the image of God has God made man" (Gen. 4:15; 9:6).

This principle of justice, known as the *lex talionis,* was codified by Moses in the following terms: "You are to take life for life, eye for eye, tooth for tooth, hand for hand, foot for foot, burn for burn, wound for wound, bruise for bruise" (Exod. 21:24). From then on, strict accounting regulated human relationships and one's relationship to God.

Today, our customs are less rigid. Of the law of retaliation, our legislators have retained only provisions concerning liability.[11] Israel, however, could not rid itself of its peculiar election. It existed for a moral purpose. God had said, "You shall be to me a holy nation." Much more was required, therefore, of the Jews than of the other nations. They had to give an account for every sin before it could be erased.[12]

Israel was also marked by God's law in its relations with other nations. No compromises were allowed. Yahweh ordered the destruction of non-Jews living in the land. "Otherwise, they will teach you to follow all the detestable things they do in worshipping their gods, and you will sin against the Lord your God" (Deut. 20:16–18). The Pharisees of Jesus' time continued to observe this law to some extent when they ordered the Jews to avoid all contact with pagans or Samaritans (John 4:9). They acted this way to save their people from idolatrous contamination. Even in Jesus' day the people of Israel were ready to use holy violence as soon as the purity of worship was desecrated. We even know of one inscription that threatened death for any pagan who dared venture into the court of the temple.

The Christian faith, rooted in the Jewish mindset, does not deny the necessity of sacred violence – far from it. But this violence has assumed a different form, thanks to the person of the *goel*.

Who is the *goel?* He is the "avenger of blood." According to the Law of Moses, if someone had been murdered, the *goel* had the responsibility of carrying out the vendetta against the guilty person. "The avenger of blood shall put the murderer to death; when he meets him, he shall put him to death" (Num. 35:19). The *goel* was the victim's next of kin. He was also the appointed protector of his relatives. If an indebted kinsman were forced to sell his land, the Book of Leviticus decreed, "his nearest relative (*goel*) is to come and redeem what his countryman has sold" (Lev. 25:25). The *goel* is thus closely intertwined with the ideas of vengeance and redemption.

The *goel* was also expected to marry the wife of his deceased kinsman as well as redeem a kinsman who had become enslaved. "If one of your countrymen becomes poor and sells himself…one of his relatives may redeem him, an uncle or a cousin or any blood relative" (Lev. 25:47ff.).

In Isaiah and the Psalms the *goel* often refers to God himself, with the double meaning of avenger and redeemer of the people of whom he is the kinsman. "Leave Babylon, flee from the Babylonians! Announce this with shouts of joy and proclaim it…The Lord has redeemed (*ga'al*) his servant Jacob" (Isa. 48:20). "Fear not, for I have redeemed you; I have summoned you by name; you are mine. When you pass through the waters, I will be with you; and when you pass through the rivers, they will not sweep over you… For I am the Lord your God, the Holy One of Israel, your Savior. I give Egypt for your ransom, Cush and Seba in your stead. Since you are precious and honored in my sight, and because I love you, I will give men in exchange for you, and people in exchange for your life" (Isa. 43:1ff.). The payment of a ransom is never omitted from the duties of the *goel*.

In Isaiah, chapters 52 and 53, another idea of *goel* appears: he is the one who redeems Israel by taking upon himself the chastisement of God. For the Christian, the figure of the "Servant of Yahweh," who gives his life in ransom for the guilty ones fallen into slavery, now thrusts itself upon Jesus (Mark 10:45). In this way the law of retaliation was transmuted. Its demand for justice, for holiness, could never be abolished. But God's vengeance would now be borne by God himself, by the God who is the *goel* of his people in the person of his Son.

Jesus believed he was the *goel,* that is, the instrument chosen by God to carry out redemption. When Jesus healed a woman with a deformed back in the synagogue, the ruler of the synagogue became indignant because Jesus had healed someone on the Sabbath, and he told the people, "There are six days for work. So come and be healed on those days, not on the Sabbath." But Jesus answered back, "You hypocrites! Doesn't each of you on the Sabbath untie his ox or donkey from the stall and lead it out to give it water? Then should not this woman, a daughter of Abraham, whom Satan has kept bound for eighteen long years, be set free on the Sabbath day from what bound her?" (Luke 13:14–16).

In all these ways – Israel's sense of election, humanity's moral foundation, and the divine requirements of justice and redemption – it is clear that Jesus' identity and mission were rooted in Hebrew thought. Jesus' theology was Jewish and he expressed it in the fundamental paradox that generates action. If God is all-powerful, nothing that happens is outside his ultimate will. But if God is good, he cannot be the author of evil and death; on the contrary, he is fighting them until the final victory.

Jesus' moral monotheism thus leads to a pragmatic dualism. We use the term "pragmatic" because Jesus, who struggled with evil, did not revere evil. However, the reality of evil, the frightening influence it has over the world, and the power it possesses over the children of God posed the problem of violence for Jesus. As he saw it, evil truly was an enemy of God, and a dangerous one, to be fought at any cost. As we shall see, only the bloody struggle of the cross and redemption was to overcome this enemy and submit it to God's order.

The basis of Jesus' behavior and thinking is quite different from ours, which is inspired mostly by scientific rationalism. And this should concern us all the more. Is modern Christianity still close enough to Judaism, still asymmetrical enough to get our rationalism-infested Western civilization out of trouble? Are we able to recognize the radical nature of Jesus' prophetic call? That is the question.

CHAPTER TWO

Jesus Proclaims Jubilee

A t the beginning of his public ministry, Jesus the prophet gave an extremely important speech in the synagogue of his hometown, Nazareth. Matthew and Mark offer but a brief summary of this event, but Luke's account is quite detailed. Here it is in its entirety:

> Jesus went to Nazareth, where he had been brought up, and on the Sabbath day he went into the synagogue, as was his custom. And he stood up to read. The scroll of the prophet Isaiah was handed to him. Unrolling it, he found the place where it is written:
>
> "The Spirit of the Lord is on me,
>   because he has anointed me
>   to preach good news to the poor.
> He has sent me to proclaim freedom for the prisoners
>   (and recovery of sight for the blind,)[1]
>   to release the oppressed,
>   to proclaim the year of the Lord's favor."
>
> Then he rolled up the scroll, gave it back to the attendant and sat down. The eyes of everyone in the synagogue were fastened on him, and he began by saying to them, "Today this scripture is fulfilled in your hearing."
>   All spoke well of him and were amazed at the gracious words that came from his lips. "Isn't this Joseph's son?" they asked. Jesus

said to them, "Surely you will quote this proverb to me: 'Physician, heal yourself! Do here in your hometown what we have heard that you did in Capernaum.'"

"I tell you the truth," he continued, "no prophet is accepted in his hometown. I assure you that there were many widows in Israel in Elijah's time, when the sky was shut for three and a half years and there was a severe famine throughout the land. Yet Elijah was not sent to any of them, but to a widow in Zarephath in the region of Sidon. And there were many in Israel with leprosy in the time of Elisha the prophet, yet not one of them was cleansed – only Naaman the Syrian."

All the people in the synagogue were furious when they heard this. They got up, drove him out of the town, and took him to the brow of the hill on which the town was built, in order to throw him down the cliff. But he walked right through the crowd and went on his way.

Then he went down to Capernaum, a town in Galilee, and on the Sabbath began to teach the people. They were amazed at his teaching, because his message had authority. (Luke 4:16–32)

This narrative deserves commenting on at length. First, although Matthew and Mark place this incident later in Jesus' ministry, Luke, who spends more effort in chronological research, places it at the beginning of Jesus' public activity, following the temptation and a first preaching tour in the synagogues. We will follow Luke's chronology.[2] It was indeed logical and congruent with the Old Testament pattern for the Spirit-filled Jesus to begin his ministry in his hometown and to try to secure the adherence of his own people to the kingdom of God. Moreover, in Matthew 4:12–13 these words follow the account of the temptation: "When Jesus heard that John had been put in prison, he returned to Galilee. Leaving Nazareth, he went and lived in Capernaum, which was by the lake." John 2:12 also places the trip to Capernaum at the beginning of Jesus' ministry, though he does not mention the dramatic events of Nazareth. All this agrees quite well with Luke's account.

Second, the part of Jesus' speech beginning with the words, "Surely you will quote this proverb to me: 'Physician, heal yourself!'" set off a wave of anger that drove Jesus from the synagogue and provoked an attempted assassination. But one cannot immediately see why Jesus would have wanted to offend his fellow kinsmen if they had not already disbelieved the beginning of his speech. Matthew and Mark also present the succession of events in this light.

Third, even under these circumstances, it is hard to understand why some of Jesus' listeners reacted with such explosive violence while others displayed astonishment and even enthusiasm. It would have taken more than a few comments about the widow of Zarephath or about Naaman the Syrian to initiate the attempt to kill Jesus. According to Jewish law only certain crimes, such as blasphemy against God or violations of the Sabbath, deserved the death penalty. But Jesus had committed none of these offenses. Perhaps he had threatened the life or interests of a part of Nazareth's population. This is what we must now investigate.

A Revolution

The passage Jesus read from Isaiah 61 gives us the answer. Here the Messiah, the Anointed One, speaks in first person: "The Lord has anointed me." Jesus chose to read precisely this passage in the synagogue of his youth, before his parents and friends. And he added, "Today this scripture is fulfilled in your hearing." In other words, to our knowledge, Jesus officially acknowledged for the first time that he was the Messiah whom the prophets had announced.[3] It is now easy to understand the amazement of some and the offense of others.

But this messianic proclamation alone could not have aroused such murderous anger. There had been others besides Jesus who made similar claims. The rest of the passage from Isaiah helps to explain it.

The Messiah announced by the prophets was the liberator. People believed he would reestablish the legitimate Davidic dynasty and free the people from foreign domination. Isaiah 61 refers to a specific liberation, and it is a social one: "To preach good news to the poor...to proclaim freedom for the captives and release for the prisoners, to proclaim the year of the Lord's favor." Being the hoped-for Messiah, Jesus meant to accomplish what the prophet announced as the task of the Messiah. He was setting out to liberate the oppressed[4] of Israel. He was proclaiming a "year of freedom" ("the year of the Lord's favor" or the "acceptable year of the Lord").

We now hold the key to the problem. By proclaiming a "year of freedom" in Nazareth, Jesus was threatening the interests of property owners, those with power. This is what incited their murderous anger. His adversaries never admitted the real motives behind their fear and hate. As good conservatives do, they hid behind noble pretexts to discredit the prophet from Nazareth. They wanted to defend certain institutions, the temple in Jerusalem, and the tradition of their fathers.[5] They resisted the "year of the Lord's favor."

Exactly what was this "year of the Lord's favor" that Jesus proclaimed? Most exegetes agree that it was nothing less than the sabbatical year or Jubilee instituted by Moses.[6]

Moses had instituted a genuine social revolution aimed at preventing the accumulation of capital in the hands of a few. This was to recur every seven and every forty-nine years. I use the term "revolution" intentionally because the social readjustments commanded by Moses were far more radical than the efforts of modern revolutionaries. Contemporary revolutions grow primarily out of economic disparities caused by technological developments. Jesus' revolution, on the contrary, drew its strength from God's liberating justice. By proclaiming the Jubilee, Jesus wanted to bring about a total social transformation, with an eye to the future, yet based on the vision of justice God had already set forth in the past.

The Jubilee, with it practices and norms, would have been known to both the poor and the rich of Nazareth. Was not the Law of Moses read every Sabbath in the synagogue? But it was not being fully put into practice. Here Jesus suddenly demanded that the Law be put into immediate effect – "today."[7] Was this good news or bad? That depended on who you were. The Jubilee demanded, among other things, expropriating the lands of the wealthy and liquidating the usurious system by which the ruling class prospered. It is easy enough to understand the enthusiasm of the poor, as well as the fear of the rich, which prompted them to try to stop this social revolution by means of a crime. Before specifying the details of the jubilean provisions and regulations, it would be good to explain the meaning of certain terms used to describe the Jubilee, which help to reveal its radical social significance. When Jesus quoted Isaiah, the jubilean connotations of these words would not have been not lost on his listeners.

The Language of Jubilee

Isaiah speaks of the "year of the Lord's favor" (Luke 4:19 – Isa. 61:2). The adjective "favorable," in Hebrew *ratson*, comes from the verb *ratsah*, which means either "to pay a debt" when it refers to the person paying it, or "to be favorable" when it refers to God accepting the payment. The Revised Standard Version uses "acceptable year," which points to the double meaning of *ratson*. For example, in Leviticus 26:41, we read, "Then [when they are in exile] when their uncircumcised hearts are humbled and they pay for their sin," and further on (v. 43), "For the land will be deserted by them and will enjoy its Sabbaths [it will lie fallow to compensate for all the unobserved sabbatical years]…and they will pay (*ratsah*) for their sins."[8] Here payment of debt is in view. Other passages, however, emphasize favor and acceptance.[9] In the passage quoted by Jesus, the Messiah proclaims, "The Lord has anointed me to...proclaim the year of the Lord's favor (a year of acceptance, or *ratson*) and the day of vengeance of our God." Jesus stops the quote with "the Lord's favor," but for Isaiah, the God "of vengeance" and the God "of mercy" are one and the same, in whom there is no contradiction.[10] In this context the "year of favor" proclaimed by Jesus involved a judgment as well as a pardon or the forgiveness of God. This was the content of the good news.

The passage in Isaiah also refers to "freedom." "The Lord has anointed me...to proclaim freedom to the captives." The Hebrew word *derôr*, which means literally "liberty," is also found in Leviticus 25:10: "Consecrate the fiftieth year and proclaim liberty throughout the land to all its inhabitants. It shall be a jubilee for you." Ezekiel 46:17 also calls the Jubilee the "year of freedom." This strongly suggests that *derôr* was used as a technical term referring to the periodic liberation of slaves as prescribed by Moses.[11]

Closely related is the idea of "release." This word (*shemittah*, in Hebrew) is found neither in Isaiah nor in Leviticus, but only in Deuteronomy (chapters 15 and 31). The verb *shamôt* means "to let alone, to let rest, to release, to remit (the payment of a debt)." *Shemittah* occurs six times in Deuteronomy 15:1–11, where it means "release, periodic cancellation of debts."[12]

In Luke's text, the Greek word *aphesis* translates both *shemittah* and *derôr*.[13] "The Lord has anointed me to proclaim *aphesis* (liberty, release) to the captives." *Aphesis* comes from the verb *aphiemi* (to send away, to liberate, to leave aside, to remit a debt). Sometimes it means "liberty," or better, the "liberation" of a slave, sometimes, "the remittance of a debt."

This word occurs quite frequently in the Gospels both as a substantive and as a verb. For instance, when John the Baptist preached the baptism of repentance it was for the release of sins considered as debts (Mark 1:4).[14] Later, referring to the healing of the paralytic, Jesus stated, "The Son of Man has authority on earth to forgive (*aphiemi*) sins" (Matt. 9:6). For the Messiah, the jubilean remission of debts extended to all areas of life—material, moral, and social. In the parable of the unforgiving servant, Jesus portrays God as a king who remits (*aphiemi*) debts acquired by his servant (Matt. 18:27–32). In the Sermon on the Mount, Jesus advises us to also "let go" or "remit" our cloak to him who wants our coat (Matt. 5:40).[15]

The jubilean significance of *aphesis* in the first three Gospels is beyond doubt. Peter, Andrew, James, and John, when called by Jesus, "left everything (*aphientes panta*) and followed him" (Luke 5:11). Shortly before Jesus' final entry into Jerusalem, the apostles happily reminded him that they had put the jubilean ordinance into practice as soon as they had heard his call: "We have left everything (*aphekamen panta*) to follow you! What then will there be for us?" (Matt. 19:27). And Jesus told them that their obedience meets God's generous jubilean initiative: "No one who has left (*apheken*) home or brothers or sisters or mother or father or children or fields for me and the gospel will fail to receive a hundred times as much in this present age (homes, brothers, sisters, mothers, children, and fields—and with them, persecutions), and in the age to come, eternal life" (Mark 10: 29–30).

Finally, Jesus uses the same word during the Last Supper, where the Jubilee is announced in eschatological terms: "This is my blood of the covenant which is poured out for many for the forgiveness (*aphesis*) of sins. I tell you, I shall not drink of this fruit of the vine from now on until that day when I drink it anew with you in my Father's kingdom" (Matt. 26:28–29). The supreme Sabbath celebrated in the kingdom of God is thus announced by a terrestrial Jubilee that foreshadows it.

In addition to the above language of freedom and release there is the notion of restoration. The word "jubilee" itself (*yobel,* in

Hebrew) does not seem to have had any particular meaning. The *yobel* was probably the ram's horn used in the land every forty-nine years on the Day of Atonement, the tenth day of the seventh month, to proclaim the beginning of the year of Jubilee. Later, it became associated with the Latin word *jubilum* (from *jubilare,* to rejoice, to exult), but this was merely a verbal coincidence. Philo of Alexandria, a contemporary of Jesus, rightly designated the Jubilee by the term *apokatastasis.* This word means to reestablish something or somebody to his previous state, a restoration or restitution of prisoners or hostages, for example. This is a subject to which Philo devotes several chapters throughout his works (cf. his *Decalogue*) and it squares beautifully with the basic meaning of the Jubilee. The very purpose of the Jubilee was to "reestablish" the tribes of Israel as they were at the time they entered Canaan.

The New Testament itself uses *apokatastasis* several times to express the idea of restoration. For instance, it can mean the reestablishment or "recovery" of a sick person.[16] In Matthew 17:11, referring to the messianic "restoration" of the kingdom of Israel, Jesus said, "Elijah comes and will restore all things." In Acts 1:6 the disciples asked Jesus, "Lord, are you at this time going to restore the kingdom to Israel?" And later in Acts Peter, quoting Deuteronomy 18:15–19, declares, "Jesus must remain in heaven until the time comes for God to restore everything, as he promised long ago through his holy prophets. For Moses said, 'The Lord your God will raise up for you a prophet like me from among your own people…'" (Acts 3:21–22).

In the last passage, Peter describes Jesus as a second Moses, who will once again enforce the ancient ordinances. Moses' return and consequently the reestablishment of the Jubilee through repentance and remission of sins are described as the condition for the great restoration when Jesus returns. Whether referring to the healing of persons or the reestablishment of the king, *apokatastasis* should be understood as having jubilean connotations. The restoration of the sick, the reestablishment of Israel, and the reestablishment of property were all part of the Messiah's redemptive task. Jesus' mission was one of jubilee!

Jubilean Provisions

The year of Jubilee was celebrated every forty-nine years, that is every seventh Sabbath of years (seven times seven).[17] Just as the week ended with a "day of release" called the Sabbath and a "week of years" ended with a sabbatical year (every seventh year), each period of forty-nine years ended with a Year of Jubilee.

Why the Year of Jubilee? What were the religious principles upon which the Year of Jubilee was based? We can identify two basic rationales.

First, God is the owner of the land. In Leviticus 25:23 we read, "The land shall not be sold permanently, because the land is mine and you are but aliens and my tenants." In the ancient world, such a declaration was not unique. The land, along with the flocks, constituted the only source of capital, and its possession guaranteed wealth and power. As a general rule, the land belonged to the god of the area or country. In practice this meant that it belonged either to the priests of the god or to the king who incarnated the god, as in Egypt. The situation was then somewhat similar to modern socialist states: the king granted the use of his lands to whomever he pleased.

But the remarkable thing about the Jubilee was that it did not lead to this type of state collectivism. On the contrary, the jubilean provisions limited the arbitrariness of the sovereign.[18] Furthermore, the interval between Jubilees did not paralyze individual initiative. It gave everyone the opportunity to invest his capital and to buy and sell goods.[19]

The redistribution of land also prevented the accumulation of capital in the hands of a few. At the time of the Jubilee every tribe repossessed the land it had received when the people of Israel first settled in Canaan. Similarly, each family regained the lands it might have lost in the interval. In this way, even though God was the ultimate owner of the land, he did not operate as a tyrant oppressing his people in slavery. Rather, he acted as a good master, entrusting to his servants the administration of his goods, which he let them enjoy, but whom he would call to account at regular intervals and once again distribute the capital he alone possessed.

Second, God is the liberator and redeemer of his people. The Jubilee is but a social and concrete rendition of God's redemptive act. "I am the Lord your God, who brought you out of Egypt to give you the land of Canaan…" (Lev. 25:38). Because God set Israel free from Egyptian bondage, social liberation (from debts, from slavery, from oppression) is to have the force of law among his people. Deuteronomy justifies the institution of the Sabbath in this way: "The seventh day is a Sabbath to the Lord your God… Remember that you were slaves in Egypt and that the Lord your God brought you out of there with a mighty hand and an outstretched arm. Therefore the Lord your God has commanded you to observe the Sabbath day" (Deut. 5:14–15).

Consequently, the mercy that manifests itself during the "year of favor" is not arbitrary. It is not the result of the king's despotic benevolence. Nor does it contradict the requirements of justice, which characterize Yahweh's will for his people. It is, rather, an expression of God's justice, which occurs at regular intervals to regularize his relations with his people. Israel's debt to God will not stack up indefinitely; accordingly, debts between fellow Israelites must also be cancelled periodically.

The following rules summarize how the sabbatical year and the Jubilee were to be celebrated:

First Measure–Every seventh year the land was to lie fallow. By a special blessing of Yahweh, the land would produce a double harvest during the sixth year.

Second Measure–During the seventh year all debts between Hebrews were to be cancelled.

Third Measure–After six years of slavery every Hebrew slave was to be set free by his master.

Fourth Measure (reserved for the Jubilee, every 49 years)–Each family was to regain possession of the land and houses it had lost in the meantime. Between two Jubilees a buyer owned the land only temporarily. As the Year of Jubilee approached, the value of the land dropped in proportion to the remaining years of tenure.

Jubilean Practice

It seems that the sabbatical year proved too difficult to apply and was therefore often ignored. This could well be the prime motive behind the year of Jubilee. The economic life of the land would have been paralyzed by the recurrence every seven years of a measure as radical as the abolition of debts or the freeing of slaves. Nevertheless, the year of Jubilee, with its additional requirement of land redistribution, does not seem to have been followed any more closely than the sabbatical year.[20]

After the return from exile, both the Mishnah and the Talmud justified the neglect of the more rigid sabbatical and jubilean measures with various unconvincing arguments. Actually, the sabbatical year and the Jubilee had already faced opposition from the ownership classes before the exile. In vain the prophets of Israel demanded the restoration of these institutions, which they saw as precursory signs of the coming of David's reign. Unfortunately, unfaithfulness usually got the upper hand. The two most remarkable attempts at restoring the Jubilee, namely those of Jeremiah and Nehemiah, are relevant here.

Under the reign of Zedekiah, the last king of Judah (598–587 B.C.), the rich had agreed to free their Hebrew slaves according to the Jubilee ordinance but soon regretted their decision and took them back. Their disobedience aroused Jeremiah's indignation, and he prophesied that it would cause the destruction of Jerusalem.

> Then the word of the Lord came to Jeremiah: "This is what the Lord, the God of Israel, says: I made a covenant with your fore-fathers when I brought them out of Egypt, out of the land of slavery. I said, 'Every seventh year each of you must free any fellow Hebrew who has sold himself to you. After he has served you six years, you must let him go free.' Your fathers, however, did not listen to me or pay attention to me. Recently you repented and did what is right in my sight: Each of you proclaimed freedom to his countrymen. You even made a covenant before me in the house that bears my Name. But now you have turned around and profaned my name; each of you has taken back the male and female slaves you had set free to go where they wished. You have forced them to become your slaves again.
>
> "Therefore, this is what the Lord says: You have not obeyed me; you have not proclaimed freedom for your fellow countrymen. So I now proclaim 'freedom' for you, declares the Lord – 'freedom' to fall by the sword, plague and famine. I will make you abhorrent to all the kingdoms of the earth." (Jer. 34:13–17)

The second attempted reform the Old Testament mentions was undertaken by Nehemiah after the return from exile, around 423 B.C. (Nehemiah 5).[21] Having called the leading citizens of Jerusalem together, Nehemiah rebuked them for requiring the poor to pawn their sons and daughters in order to eat and stay alive. And he tells them, "Give back to them immediately their fields, vineyards, olive groves, and houses, and also the usury you are charging them – the hundredth part of the money, grain, new wine, and oil." And they said, "We will give it back…and we will not demand any-thing more from them." However, the last chapters of Isaiah, as well as of Ezekiel, still count the Jubilee among the institutions to be reestablished.

A few additional remarks will help us better understand the scope of the jubilean ordinances. According to Deuteronomy 15, slaves were set free after seven years of service. This liberation did not necessarily coincide with the sabbatical year. It should also be noted that the freed slaves were Hebrew. The jubilean ordinances did not apply to foreigners. The Jews had no obligation to free the foreign slaves they might have owned. Loans with interest were also forbidden among Jews but could be made to foreigners in matters of trade. A Jew could also require the reimbursement of a debt from a foreigner, in spite of the Jubilee.

These distinctions which the Mosaic Law made between Jews and foreigners belong to the background of the Gospels. In a later chapter, we will examine Jesus' struggle to abolish them.

It should be noted, however, that the Roman or Oriental type of slavery was nonexistent among the Jews. Slavery for the Jews was a consequence of mortgages taken by a creditor on the lands of an insolvent debtor. The creditor could use the lands until their revenue had paid off the amount of the debt. If this did not suffice he could require the debtor (with his wife and children) to work for him until the entire debt had been paid off. This resulted in a form of effective slavery, which was still practiced in Jesus' time. If a Jubilee occurred, the "slave" would be ipso facto freed, since all debts were cancelled, and he could regain his ownership rights.

In Jesus' time, a period we will study in more depth in the next chapter, the situation could be summed up as follows: The anonymous author of the Book of Jubilees, as well as Philo of Alexandria, attached merely ritual significance to the Jubilee. It was limited to celebrating the days, months, and years, according to an orthodox calendar. On the other hand, the Pharisaic rabbis recommended the observance of sabbatical years, while simultaneously trying to attenuate their strictness. Letting the land lie fallow every seventh year was the sole surviving sabbatical practice obeyed by the people.

Certain historical events prove that this practice was still observed, at least to some extent. According to the First Book of the Maccabees 6:48–53, the Jews who in 162 B.C. had given up defending Beth-zur against Lysias's Syrian troops were also forced to abandon the defense of Mount Zion. "They had no food in storage, because it was the seventh year; those who had found safety in Judea from the Gentiles had consumed the last of the stores." The historian Flavius Josephus reports the same event.[22]

Josephus refers to two other famines that were aggravated by sabbatical years: one in 135–134 B.C., which occurred during the siege of the Dagon Fortress by John Hyrcanus, and the other in 38–37 B.C., when Herod the Great was besieging Antigonus in Jerusalem. While these dates don't exactly fit the sabbatical calendar,[23] after Christ the chronology becomes more precise.

We know, for example, that A.D. 47–48 marked the beginning of a great famine, which affected the whole empire. This was the famine announced by Agabus in Acts 11:28. In Palestine it was aggravated by the return of the sabbatical year. According to the *Sotah* tractate of the Mishnah (VII, 8), the preceding sabbatical year had been celebrated with particular solemnity by Herod Agrippa I, grandson of Herod the Great. He is the Herod mentioned in Acts 12, to whom Emperor Claudius, out of gratitude, had given back the entire kingdom of his grandfather in A.D. 41.

To please the Jews, Herod Agrippa persecuted the Christians (he beheaded James, the brother of John) and practiced the Jewish religion with ostentation. In A.D. 41 he publicly read the Law of Moses to mark the end of the sabbatical year, as prescribed in Deuteronomy 31:10. Having gathered the people in Jerusalem, he began to read but broke out in tears when he came

to Deuteronomy 17:15: "He must be from among your own brothers. Do not place a foreigner over you, one who is not a brother
Israelite." In fact, the Herodians were Idumaeans, and therefore
foreign to Israel. But the people reassured the king by shouting,
"You are our brother, you are our brother!" because they were
quite fond of Agrippa.

This story is of great interest for our chronology because it
enables us to set A.D. 26–27 (two septennials earlier) as the date
of the sabbatical year Jesus inaugurated in the synagogue of Nazareth. It would then have been in A.D. 26, on the tenth day of the
month of Tishri, which is the Day of Atonement (*Yom Kippur*),
that Jesus announced the complete restoration of the jubilean
practices in Israel. We say "jubilean practices" because, as we have
seen, the ordinances of the sabbatical year and of the Jubilee coincided. The calendar of jubilean years was subject to controversy
even among the Jews, making it hard for us to recreate it with
accuracy.[24]

Two centuries after Jesus, the orthodox Jews who remained in
Palestine still observed the sabbatical year. Rabbi Abrabu recalls
the way some Gentiles made fun of Jews. They would bring an
emaciated camel to the theater and rail, "Why is this camel so
afflicted? Because the Jews are observing their sabbatical year, and
since they have run out of vegetables, they are eating the plants
this camel used for food."

When Jesus proclaimed good news to the poor, liberty to the
captives, and sight to the blind, his audience knew very well what
he meant: now is the time to put into effect the year of Jubilee.
Jesus' speech in Nazareth was no sermon of religious platitudes.
He was announcing that a social revolution was underway – the
messianic reign had begun. For the poor, this was good news. All
things would be made right again. For those whose interests were

vested in the establishment, however, such news was a threat. Was Jesus serious? How far did he plan to take all this? Where would it lead?

CHAPTER THREE

Implications of Jubilee

The speech at Nazareth alone would not be enough to prove that Jesus proclaimed a Jubilee. A more complete reading of the Gospels is needed to validate our thesis. As we have just seen, the Jubilee or sabbatical year prescribed four provisions: letting the land lie fallow, the remittance of debts, the liberation of slaves, and the redistribution of capital. This chapter will explore further references in the Gospels to these four provisions.[1]

The Fallow Year

Jesus does not directly mention the provision of letting the land lie fallow. His silence on the subject is not surprising, since this sabbatical prescription was the only one already accepted by the people. It was therefore unnecessary to encourage the Jews to put it into practice. But they surely needed courage to let their land lie fallow every seventh year while counting on God to give them what they needed. In Leviticus 25:20–21 Yahweh foresaw their uneasiness and declared, "You may ask, 'What will we eat in the seventh year if we do not plant or harvest our crops?' I will send you such a blessing in the sixth year that the land will yield enough for three years."

Jesus talked to his disciples in similar terms. His proclamation of the Jubilee may have troubled them because they had abandoned their land and their boats by the lake to follow him. "So do not worry, saying, 'What shall we eat?' or 'What shall we drink?' or 'What shall we wear?' For the pagans run after all these things, and your heavenly Father knows that you need them. But seek first his kingdom and his righteousness, and all these things will be given to you as well" (Matt. 6:31–33).

Such an exhortation might be misunderstood as encouraging laziness, but in the framework of expecting God's kingdom (of which the Jubilee was to be a foretaste) it can easily be explained. One can interpret Jesus' exhortation as follows: "If you work six days (or six years) with all your heart you can count on God to take care of you and your loved ones. Let your land lie fallow without fear. Just as he does for the birds of the sky, who neither sow nor reap nor gather away in barns, God will also provide for your needs. The Gentiles who ignore the Sabbath are no richer than you are."

Remittance of Debt and Liberation of Slaves

Unlike the preceding regulation, the second and third jubilean provisions are not marginal, but central to Jesus' teaching, even to his theological vision.

The Lord's Prayer, which sums up Jesus' thinking about prayer, contains the following request: "Forgive (or remit) us our debts as we also have forgiven our debtors." Several versions translate this passage incorrectly as: "Forgive us our trespasses as we forgive those who trespass against us." In reality, the Greek *opheilema* means a money debt, a sum owed, in the material sense of the word.[2] Jesus is not vaguely recommending that we forgive those who have created problems for us. No, he is instructing us to forgive sins, which includes completely canceling the debts of those who owe us money, that is, to practice the Jubilee.

The material connotation of the word "debts" in the Lord's Prayer was so obvious that Jesus thought it fitting to add a commentary to the prayer, to explain that the words concerning the debts also applied to "trespasses" in general: "For if you forgive men when they sin against you, your heavenly Father will also forgive you. But if you do not forgive men their sins [the term he uses here is *paraptoma,* or transgression], your Father will not forgive your sins" (Matt. 6:14–15).

Thus, the Lord's Prayer is truly jubilean. In this context, Jesus' listeners understood it to mean: "The time has come for God's people to cancel all the debts that bind the poor because their debts to God have also been cancelled." Jesus was setting up a rigorous equation between practicing the Jubilee and the grace of God. Although he was not otherwise a legalist and unhesitatingly forgave even prostitutes and people of ill repute, Jesus was very strict on this one point: only he who grants forgiveness can be forgiven. God's *aphesis* toward you is in vain if you do not practice *aphesis* toward others.[3]

The parable of the unmerciful servant and the parable of the unjust steward both further clarify Jesus' thought on this point. The first expresses the strictness of the "equation" of the Lord's Prayer: no mercy for him who has none (Matt. 18:21–35).

Why has this parable been detached from its sociological background? Why has it been understood as a rather pale portrayal of the forgiveness of sins granted by God to those who forgive their brothers? In fact, its sorry hero was almost certainly a real person, a Galilean peasant whose name was probably known to Jesus' disciples. He had been a beneficiary of the proclamation of the Jubilee, having been granted forgiveness by God. All his debts had been cancelled, though they were enormous: 10,000 talents (approximately ten million dollars!). This astronomical figure expresses the debtor's insolvency toward the prince.

We now know how Galilean peasants who had been free proprietors before Jesus' time had been forced into slavery by their
progressive indebtedness. To a large extent, Herod the Great was
to blame for this situation. He had overburdened the people
with taxes and expropriated the recalcitrant proprietors. To avoid
expropriation, a peasant borrowed money from a usurer who
usually worked hand in hand with the king's steward or the tax
collector. His pawned property would soon become the usurer's,
and the peasant his sharecropper, or "servant." But this did not
solve the peasant's problems. His unpaid debts accumulated until
they reached horrendous proportions. The creditor sought repay-
ment and ordered that the sharecropper be sold (along with his
wife, children, and all he owned) in order to reimburse the debt.
This was the situation of the "unforgiving servant." Jesus described
the peasant's loss of his property and freedom as a direct consequence of his indebtedness.

But because of the Jubilee, the servant appears before the king,
who cancels his debt. This story would be quite encouraging if
it stopped there. But it was told at a time when Jesus was facing
opposition to the Jubilee from the majority of his fellow Jews,
sometimes even from very humble ones. The rest of the story
reflects his bitter disappointment in the face of this rejection.

Upon meeting one of his fellow servants, who owed him about
twenty-five dollars, the newly freed slave refuses to grant his debtor
the same jubilean privilege that set him free. He seizes him by the
throat and says, "Pay what you owe." Denounced by his fellow
servants, the unforgiving servant is arrested and taken before the
king. The Jubilee is no longer applicable for such an unmerciful
and thankless man. He must be sold along with his wife and children to pay for his debts. There is no divine Jubilee for those who
refuse to practice it on earth.

The jubilean practice of forgiving debts had one very serious
drawback, which is addressed in Deuteronomy 15:7–11. A too

frequent occurrence of the remittance of debts tended to freeze credit. As the sabbatical year approached the rich were increasingly hesitant to loan money to the poor for fear of losing their capital. This stinginess paralyzed the economy and hindered their profits. Because of this, some of the most orthodox rabbis, even champions of the restoration of the Mosaic Law such as Hillel and Shammai, hesitated to require a strict application of the Jubilee.

The rabbis, and in particular Hillel, eventually came up with a solution to this problem. The solution was called the *prosbul*.[4] *Prosbul* probably comes from the Greek *pros boule* (a deed carried out before a law court). According to the *Gittin* tractate of the Mishnah (iv, 3), Hillel gave the creditor permission to use a court as his attorney in recovering a debt that the sabbatical year had abolished. By means of this subterfuge, loans with interest, which had been abolished by the Mosaic Law (Exod. 22:25) and limited in duration by the provisions of the sabbatical year, once again became possible. The rich, and particularly the Pharisees, whom Jesus accused of "devouring widows' houses," used this measure to its fullest.

The Mishnah has preserved a text which refers to the *prosbul*: "I (so and so) transfer to you (so and so), the judges (in such and such a place), my right to a debt, so that you may recover any amount which (so and so) owes me, at whatever time I will so desire." The *prosbul* was then signed by the judges and the witnesses.

Jesus was an avowed adversary of the *prosbul*. Usually, Jesus is pictured as an opponent of the sabbatical laws. But in this case, the opposite is true. When it was a question of bringing out the humanitarian intentions of the Mosaic Law, Jesus was even more radical than the Pharisees.[5] If this were not the case, Jesus' continuous confrontations with the Pharisees would lose all meaning, especially if they merely centered on religious practices. In reality, the conflict went much deeper than that. It revolved around the nature of justice.

"What is goodness?" the Pharisees would ask themselves, and they would answer with a multitude of detailed ordinances in the midst of which they lost the essential truth.

"What is goodness?" Jesus would ask. His answer was to go back to the essential thrust of the Mosaic Law, without detouring through the scribes' elaborate interpretations. Jesus' radicalism was exactly the opposite of forgoing the Law. When Jesus retorted that God made the Sabbath for man, he meant: "God set the Jews free by taking them out of Egypt. The sabbatical year, like the Sabbath, must be put into practice. It was made to set people free, not to enslave them." That is why the *prosbul,* as well as all other regulations added to the Law to alter its liberating and revolutionary character, provoked Jesus' indignation.

But the question remains: how can one avoid freezing credit if the lure of profit is taken away? In the Sermon on the Mount Jesus gave his answer. The rich must prove themselves generous by eradicating their desire to be reimbursed, because God will take the matter into his own hands.

> And if you lend to those from whom you expect repayment, what credit is that to you? Even "sinners" lend to "sinners," expecting to be repaid in full. But…lend to them without expecting to get anything back. Then your reward will be great, and you will be sons of the Most High, because he is kind to the ungrateful and wicked. Be merciful, just as your Father is merciful…Give, and it will be given to you. A good measure, pressed down, shaken together and running over, will be poured into your lap. (Luke 6:34–38)

In all this the honesty of the debtor must coincide with the generosity of the lender. The debtor should not hide behind the protection of the sabbatical year in order to escape his own obligation. Again, the Sermon on the Mount contains two striking paragraphs where Jesus points out possible solutions to the problem upon which Hillel and the Pharisees had stumbled.

Hillel would tell the worried creditor: "Take your claims to the court. Your money will be restored to you there." Jesus tells the careless debtor not to wait for a court summons to repay his debt: "If someone [your creditor] wants to sue you [using the *prosbul*] and take your tunic⁶ [which he holds as a pledge for the debt you have not repaid], let him have your cloak as well" (Matt. 5:40). Prior to this, Jesus advises, "Settle matters quickly with your adversary who is taking you to court. Do it while you are still with him on the way, or he [using the *prosbul*] may hand you over to the judge, and the judge may hand you over to the officer, and you may be thrown into prison. I tell you the truth, you will not get out until you have paid the last penny" (Matt. 5:25). According to the parallel passage in Luke 12:52–59, Jesus asks, "Why don't you judge for yourselves what is right?" His disciples should avoid court proceedings altogether. Why should they rely on the courts to decide whether or not it is right to pay their debts?⁷

The other parable with a jubilean teaching, the parable of the dishonest steward (Luke 16:1–9), also revolves around the peasants' status in Jesus' time. Due to the extortions of King Herod–as well as those of his son and the Roman occupant–most of the older proprietors had lost their independence. Forced to mortgage their property in order to pay their taxes, they had been driven into semi-slavery. The taxes in oil and wheat that they paid to their masters often amounted to half or more of their harvest.

The peasants' conditions in Israel were aggravated by yet another evil: the owners' absenteeism. A hierarchy of middlemen (toll-gatherers, publicans, customs officials, stewards, and managers) had the task of collecting debts. They extorted from the sharecropper arbitrary sums of money that exceeded the rent, debts, and taxes they actually owed. The poor were always in the wrong. They could rely on no one because the stewards presented falsified accounts to their masters. With the help of these accounts, they were able to accumulate what Jesus called "unrighteous mammon." It was by constantly seeking these unjust riches that the stewards lost their genuine riches, namely, the friendship of their fellow citizens.

This parable tells how a landowner discovered the dishonesty of his steward. Not only did the steward plunder the sharecroppers, he also stole from his master to whom he showed falsified records. Once his cheating had been discovered, the steward began to feel the pangs of conscience. He understood that he would never be able to reimburse the entire amount of his swindling. But he decided at least not to require of the sharecroppers exaggerated amounts they had not yet paid. He then erased the amount by which he had unjustly increased their debts. Jesus describes him calling the debtors together and reducing their debts to their correct amount: fifty measures of oil instead of a hundred, eighty measures of wheat instead of a hundred, etc.

Such a decision certainly increased the steward's insolvency. It forced him into poverty. But by acting as he did, he would acquire genuine riches, that is the thankfulness and friendship of his previous victims. Poor among the poor, man among men, he would be received as a brother in their homes. That, says Jesus, is the nature of God's kingdom. The point of the parable? Jesus says, "Use worldly wealth to gain friends for yourselves"(Luke 16:9). That is, put the Jubilee I'm announcing into practice. By liberating others from their debts, you set yourselves free from fetters that bind, which keep you from being ready for the coming of God's kingdom of justice.

The most remarkable part of the parable is the praise for the steward's shrewdness that Jesus puts into the mouth of the landowner, who symbolizes God. In the parable of the unforgiving servant, God is the one who takes the initiative. God is the first to cancel our debt, and so he expects us to do the same. In the parable of the dishonest steward, it is man who takes the initiative. He is the first to put the Jubilee into practice by obeying the messianic call and remitting the debts of those who are debtors to God, as well as debtors to himself. Consequently, God praises this man for practicing the redistribution of wealth even before being touched by divine grace. He was able to read the signs of God's kingdom and understand that the rule of unjust riches is over.

These two parables coincide with and confirm the inferences of the speech at Nazareth, the Lord's Prayer, and the teachings of the Sermon on the Mount. Jesus was indeed proclaiming a Jubilee, consistent with Moses' sabbatical instructions, a Jubilee capable of reversing the social problems of Israel at that time. It would abolish debts and set free the debtors whose insolvency had turned them into slaves. For Jesus, putting such a Jubilee into practice was not optional. "Forgive us our debts, as we also have forgiven our debtors" was one of the prerequisites of his kingdom. Those who refused to take heed could not enter.

The Redistribution of Capital

The Gospels clearly indicate that Jesus voluntarily accepted poverty in view of the coming kingdom. He also commanded his disciples to practice the redistribution of their capital. During the time of Jesus, land and flocks were the people's only wealth, or in today's terminology, "capital." Yet Jesus taught, "Seek his kingdom, and these things will be given to you as well. Do not be afraid, little flock, for your Father has been pleased to give you the kingdom. Sell your possessions and give to the poor" (Luke 12:31–33). Does this mean that Jesus commanded a blanket redistribution of wealth on the part of all his followers? Or did he mean it to be only a "counsel of perfection" applicable to a select number of saints at certain times?

Traditionally, the church has chosen the second interpretation, the easy one. Only the person with a particular vocation, such as the monk, is called to abandon all his possessions. The ordinary believer can be content to "give alms," that is, to distribute part of his income to the poor.

Such a position would be quite justifiable had Jesus not been so harsh toward those very people who in his own day were complacently satisfied with their almsgiving – the Pharisees. They gave one tenth of all their income, no mean accomplishment in light of the taxation requirements of the Romans. But Jesus did not believe that this was enough: "Woe to you, teachers of the law and Pharisees, you hypocrites! You give a tenth of your spices – mint, dill, and cummin. But you have neglected the more important matters of the law – justice, mercy, and faithfulness. You should have practiced the latter, without neglecting the former" (Matt. 23:23). This confirms Jesus' radicalism; he did not want to abolish the Law, but fulfill it by exercising justice, mercy, and faithfulness.

What did Jesus mean by these three words? Everything points to the fact that he meant the gratuitous act by which his disciples ceased planning for their own futures and gave away even what they needed for themselves. "Unless your righteousness surpasses that of the Pharisees and the teachers of the law, you will certainly not enter the kingdom of heaven" (Matt. 5:20).

Consider the following incident. One day, as Jesus was comparing the generosity of the rich, who ostensibly put large gifts into the offering box, and that of a poor widow, Jesus exclaimed, "This poor widow has put in more than all the others. All these people gave their gifts out of their wealth; but she out of her poverty put in all she had to live on" (Luke 21:1–4). In other words, it matters little how much one gives. What matters is what one gives. If it is just a part of your income, it isn't justice, mercy, and faithfulness.

This is not to say that Jesus prescribed some kind of socialist communism. If he had done so, he would have left with his disciples either monastic rules similar to those of the Essenes, or some constitutional order to be implemented within a collectivist

Jewish state. He did neither of these things. Forced collectivism was contrary to the spirit of the Mosaic Law, not to mention Jesus' gospel of the kingdom.

When Jesus commanded, "Sell your possessions and give to the poor" (a better translation would be, "Sell what you possess and practice kind deeds"), it was neither a counsel of perfection, nor a constitutional law founding a utopian state. It was rather a joyful announcement to be put into practice here and now in A.D. 26 as a "refreshment" foreshadowing the restitution of all things. "Give what is inside," as in Luke 11:41.

Such a redistribution of capital every forty-nine years, out of faithfulness to God's justice and in the hope of the kingdom, need not be utopian, nor forced. Many bloody revolutions might have been avoided had the Christian church alone, with all its holdings, practiced the jubilean ideal.[8]

When interpreted in light of the Jubilee, many of Jesus' other teachings fall easily into place. And none of this takes away the spiritual force of Jesus' message. For surely when Jesus announced the inauguration of the Jubilee he was also thinking about the salvation of his people. He consistently made a rigorous equation between the Jubilee practiced here on earth and the grace of God. "Sell everything you have and give to the poor, and you will have treasure in heaven" (Luke 18:22). "Sell your possessions and give to the poor. Provide purses for yourselves that will not wear out, a treasure in heaven that will not be exhausted…" (Luke 12:33).[9]

The redistribution of capital as taught in the above verses could be misconstrued to encourage selfish acts with the aim of securing one's place in heaven. The believer thus rids himself of all his possessions in order to purchase his salvation. In reality, however, compassion for the poor precedes the acquisition of treasure in heaven. What matters primarily to God is the lot of the poor. It is for them that the "rich young ruler" must sell his possessions;

doing so *is* the treasure. To practice compassion is to reestablish the poor in the condition God willed for everyone. God will, one day, entirely reestablish the poor, with or without the help of the rich. "Blessed are you who are poor, for yours is the kingdom of God." If it does not happen in this life, it will be realized in the next, as expressed in Jesus' parable of Lazarus and the rich man (Luke 16:19–31). In the end, those in a precarious situation are not the poor, but the rich who refuse to put the Jubilee into practice. If they don't distribute their capital now, it may be too late tomorrow. "Woe to you who are rich, for you have already received your comfort." A tremendous chasm separates the kingdom of God from the place where the rich like to enjoy themselves in pleasure.

The power of salvation is such that it brings with it acts of liberation. Consider the examples of two people to whom Jesus proposed a jubilean redistribution: Zacchaeus, who accepted, and the rich young ruler, who did not.

The former belonged to the scorned class of publicans and usurers whose activities are described above. Zacchaeus had become rich by lending money at usurious rates to the insolvent poor with one hand so that they could pay the government taxes he collected with the other hand. Before meeting Jesus, Zacchaeus had probably already heard rumors about his proclamation of the Jubilee. All the unjust riches he had acquired troubled Zacchaeus's conscience. The story tells us that instead of fleeing from the prophet, he climbed a tree to see him. Jesus called Zacchaeus down because he wanted to stay in his house. His sheer presence compelled Zacchaeus to see that his wealth resulted from robbery. Applying to himself the commandment of Exodus 22:1–4,[10] which tells the robber to return four for the one he stole, Zacchaeus cried out, "Look, Lord! Here and now I give half of my possessions to the poor, and if I have cheated anybody out of anything, I will pay back four times the amount" (Luke 19:1–10).

By this action Zacchaeus was joining the great movement of jubilean reform undertaken by Jesus. He was practicing what Jesus preached by abolishing his part in the system of exploitation under which the people of Israel were suffering. And so Jesus exclaimed, "Today salvation has come to this house, because this man, too, is a son of Abraham. For the Son of Man came to seek and to save what was lost." One could conclude that those who do not practice the Jubilee are excluding themselves from among the sons of Abraham.

Jesus considered the rich who did not redistribute their capital as lost. When referring to the rich young ruler, Jesus said, "How hard it is for the rich to enter the kingdom of God!" and the disciples cried out, "Who then can be saved?" Indeed, the rich young ruler had refused to sell his possessions and return them to the poor. He had received the command as the disciples had – to put the Jubilee into practice – but he had not obeyed. Despite Jesus' sympathy for him, he could not be one of his disciples (Luke 18:18–30).

The contrast between the bitter sorrow of the rich young ruler and the joy of the apostles, who had responded to Jesus' call by leaving behind all that they had, is indeed striking. It was, in fact, after the rich man's departure that Peter exclaimed, "We have left all we had to follow you!" Jesus answered, "I tell you the truth, no one who has left home or wife or brothers or parents or children for the sake of the kingdom of God will fail to receive many times as much in this age and, in the age to come, eternal life" (Luke 18:28–30).

No other text gives a better summary of Jesus' revolution. He was not concerned with the reform of certain details, but with overturning everything, including the entire economic hierarchy of society. The rich, as attached as they are to their possessions, are relegated to the last rank, whereas the "poor in spirit," who have voluntarily thrown off their possessions to fulfill the Jubilee, are now in the first rank. "Blessed are you who hunger now, for you will be satisfied…Woe to you who are well fed now, for you will go hungry" (Luke 6:21, 25). Only in light of the Jubilee can the meaning and scope of these words fully reveal themselves.

An honest reading of the Gospels confirms that Jesus was truly proclaiming a Jubilee in Nazareth.[11] The jubilean prescriptions and their implementation in concrete form had a central place both in Jesus' ethics and in his proclamation of the kingdom of God. In fact, the Jubilee was a preeminent sign of God's justice and salvation on earth. God's kingdom is here and now; it fulfills itself through years of conscientious labor followed by the year of favor that crowns the completed work with the good news of divine forgiveness.

CHAPTER FOUR

The "Politics" of Jesus

M any Christian ethicists assert that Jesus left us no political teaching. In one sense they are right. Any hope of finding in the Gospels some type of partisan politics or criticism of first-century political regimes, such as the kingdom of the Herod dynasty or the Roman Empire, is futile. Nor can a comprehensive teaching be found concerning the nature of church-state relations.

But an apolitical interpretation of the Gospels is wrong on at least two counts. First, it takes Jesus' sayings out of context. For example, Jesus says, "Give to Caesar what is Caesar's, and to God what is God's" (Matt. 22:15–22), or "You would have no power over me if it were not given to you from above" (John 19:11). From these passages exegetes mistakenly conclude that the disciple should submit humbly to the authorities and do his civil duty. Such assumptions totally stifle any attempt to apply Jesus' teachings to the social level, not to mention how they also discourage any Gospel-inspired attempts to transform social institutions.

Second, an apolitical gospel causes churchgoers to obey the established order blindly, without giving much thought to how such obedience supports oppressive regimes, such as the tyrannical dictatorships in Latin America and Africa. In short, such a gospel amounts to good news only for the rich – quite a different message from that of the One who went about proclaiming good news for the poor.

Citizenship and the Polis

If our hypothesis is correct, that Jesus came to proclaim and implement a jubilean revolution, then the apolitical view of the gospel is fundamentally wrong. Jesus' revolution is political by its very nature.[1]

In Jesus' time, the verb *politeuo* meant "to live as a citizen," that is, to live according to the laws of a city (*polis*). Joseph, for example, submitted himself to the census ordered by Emperor Augustus and went to Bethlehem, city of David, of which he was a citizen. In Acts 21:39 Paul declares, "I am a Jew, from Tarsus in Cilicia, a citizen of no ordinary city." The Roman tribune who, years later, arrested Paul in Jerusalem discovered that Paul was a Roman citizen. The commander in charge of Paul said to him, "I had to pay a big price for my citizenship," to which Paul retorted, "But I was born a citizen" (Acts 22:28). Thus Paul was simultaneously a citizen of Tarsus and of Rome.

At that time, the Roman Empire was still only a constellation of cities, submitting to Rome of course, but each forming a separate "state," a *polis* with its civil government, its laws, its institutions, its authorities, and its cults and gods (e.g., Diana of Ephesus and, from Rome's perspective, Yahweh of Jerusalem). Therefore, each of the cities Paul visited during his trips enjoyed a particular status and kept its gods, its laws, and its magistrates. Some were Roman colonies, such as Lystra, Philippi, and Troas. Others had the status of free cities, such as Tarsus, Perga, Thessalonica, Athens, and, for a time, Joppa, which Caesar later returned to the Jews. The free cities were tied to Rome by a covenant. Most of them had autonomous finances and were sometimes exempt from paying tribute to Caesar.

In the completely pacified regions Rome only maintained a small number of soldiers. On the other hand, the troubled provinces were directly under the emperor's control through an intermediary called a legate, or governor. The legate of Syria, for example, resided at Antioch. He had the procurator of Palestine, who resided in Caesarea, under his authority.

In principle, the Roman governor of the province merely served as the protector of the cities. His work was limited to regulating relations between cities, guaranteeing the judicial privileges of the local magistrates, listening to complaints against them, and forbidding religious practices that disturbed the peace.

As one can see, the framework of a Roman "nation" barely existed. In all the empire, the Jewish nation was an exception. Those of its members who had settled throughout the empire recognized only one God, the God of Jerusalem. They made a pilgrimage to the temple in Jerusalem once a year. Among the inhabitants of the pagan cities, only the Jews had managed to be exempted from sacrificing to the local gods. They were also exempted from military service because such service would violate the observance of the Sabbath.

This does not mean that Israel's religious unity extended to the political sphere. Far from it. After the death of Herod the Great, the province of Palestine was subdivided into six different territories placed under the authority of three sovereigns. Judea and Samaria, with their well-known quarrels, were directly under the authority of the Roman procurator in Caesarea. Galilee and Perea were governed by Herod Antipas. Decapolis and Trachonitis formed the tetrarchy of Philip, the brother of Herod Antipas.

Jewish cities and provinces also resisted all attempts of fusion: one was either Galilean or Judean, Samarian or Syro-Phoenician. The Gospels mention Simon "of Cyrene," Joseph "of Arimathea," Mary Magdalene (of Magdala). Hence, Jesus, a citizen of Nazareth, could not be recognized as the Messiah by Nathaniel, a citizen of Cana (John 1:46).

The historian Josephus notes that there were fifteen fortified cities in Galilee alone. There existed a similar number in the tetrarchy of Philip, in Perea, in Samaria, and in Judea. The Gospels mention Nazareth, Capernaum, Cana, Nain, Magdala, Korazin in Galilee; Bethsaida and Gadara in the tetrarchy of Philip; Sychar and Shechem in Samaria; Jericho, Ephraim, Bethlehem, Emmaus, and Jerusalem in Judea. To this list one can add the cities mentioned by Josephus: Gisehala, Gadara, Gabara, Jezreel, Pella, Bethel, Tekoa, Hebron, and so forth. Behind the walls of each city, life had a distinct political flavor.

Jesus and the Powers

The political nature of Jesus' thought did not directly apply to the problems of the Roman Empire, but rather to the cities of Israel, to which he directed his call. When he recruited his first disciples, it was with the intent of sending them as "apostles" or messengers to the cities of Israel to implore each of them, as a whole, to change its ways. Everything in them had to be transformed – institutions as well as hearts.

The fact that the proclamation of the kingdom was directed to the cities of Israel underlines the politically Jewish character of Jesus' program. Cities like Sepphoris, north of Nazareth, and Caesarea of Philippi and even Tiberias, which was at the center of Jesus' sphere of action, are not mentioned in the Gospels. Why not? They were foreign cities, founded by the Herod dynasty or by the Romans. They did not belong to the "twelve tribes of Israel." The kingdom of God was no concern of theirs.

Imagine the intense life of these communities, their streets buzzing with the vitality of a crowd of people of humble station: artisans, carpenters, fishermen, weavers, and potters. The wealthier people owned a piece of land on the outskirts of the town, planted with vines and fig and olive trees. The sons of the poor would hire themselves out as shepherds and lead the flocks to the pastures on the hilltops.

The city had both its rich and its poor—alas, more poor than rich![2] In addition to ordinary peasants, the poor included the sick, the blind, the lepers, and the crippled for whom no hospital cared. There were also the widows, who lost all their rights if a *goel* did not redeem them. They would fall victim to usurers who forced them into mortgaging their houses and sometimes even their clothes. The rich included the public officials. The Roman presence, with its garrisons at the city gate, guaranteed the security of the governor, the steward, and the publican.

The Jewish authorities, however, were located specifically in Jerusalem. The four Gospels constantly underscore the preeminence of these authorities. It was they who should have recognized the Messiah, because they represented the people. The Sanhedrin was the supreme authority, chaired by the high priest, who exercised the supreme power (*exousia*). His authority extended to the political, judicial, and religious spheres of life. Every city also had its magistrates, judge, chief tax collector, and its head of the synagogue, who was influential because he was the interpreter of Israel's theocratic traditions.

Indeed, the synagogue was the place where the lawyers taught and commented upon the Mosaic Law and where they defined the practical guidelines of its implementation. It was precisely at this level that Jesus made his political claims. When he said, "One greater than the temple is here" (Matt. 12:6), he was claiming *exousia,* the power and authority that belonged only to the legitimate authorities of Israel. When he spoke for the first time in the synagogue of Capernaum, the crowd was stupefied because "he taught them as one who had authority, not as the teachers of the law" (Mark 1:22).

It is easier to grasp the conflict between Jesus and Israel's leaders if we examine it in terms of power. The entire controversy with the scribes centered on the question of power: there could not be two legitimate powers in Israel. If Jesus was the Son of David, the legitimate king of Israel (Matt.12:23), then he had the power from God, and in this case the leaders of the people should place themselves under his authority. In Jerusalem the crowd even thought for a moment that the Jewish leaders had surrendered to him: "Have the authorities really concluded that he is the Christ?" (John 7:26). Alas, very early in the struggle the opposition prevailed. Already in Galilee the Pharisees (from whose ranks came most of the lawyers and who had come to Jerusalem to stop the messianic movement) had loudly declared that the power Jesus claimed was illegitimate. It came, they said, not from Yahweh, but from Beelzebub, the prince of demons (Luke 11:15).

No slander could have insulted Jesus more than this one, which explains his fulminating response. The disciples of the Pharisees had also been casting out demons. Jesus was quite happy about this; it meant he was not the only one announcing the coming of the kingdom of God through miracles. "Do not stop him," he had told his disciples. "Whoever is not against us is for us" (Mark 9:38–40). God's spirit ("God's finger," according to Luke) uses various means to advance the kingdom.

At this point, however, Jesus' answer to the lawyers and teachers was incisive. There is only one kingdom, one finger of God, one spirit that manifests itself in power. The kingdom cannot be divided against itself: "He who is not with me is against me" (Luke 11:17–23). By accusing me of being an instrument of Beelzebub you are giving way to pure jealousy; you are knowingly sinning against the spirit of God. And anyone who speaks against the Holy Spirit will not be forgiven (Matt. 12:31–32).

Thus Jesus was claiming for himself all power and authority, be it religious, social, political, or otherwise. There could be no compromise. He demanded to be recognized by the leaders of the cities of Israel as the Son of David and king of Israel.[3]

When we grasp Jesus' confrontation with the powers, we can better understand the nature of the message he entrusted to his apostles.[4] It had a decisively political character.[5] Jesus saw each city of Israel as a political entity and, in turn, called each one as a whole to repentance. To the very end he spoke to the city as a whole: "O Jerusalem, Jerusalem, you who kill the prophets and stone those sent to you, how often I have longed to gather your children together, as a hen gathers her chicks under her wings, but you were not willing! Look, your house is left to you desolate" (Luke 13:34–35). In sending out his disciples, it is clear that Jesus believed in the possibility of a collective and sudden repentance of each city in Israel. Why else did he order his disciples to remain in each city long enough to tell the inhabitants about the good news of the imminent kingdom? (Matt. 10:23).

Jesus' message took the form of an ultimatum. The cities of Israel had to decide on the spot for or against the kingdom of God.

> When you enter a town and are welcomed, eat what is set before you. Heal the sick who are there and tell them, "The kingdom of God is near you." But when you enter a town and are not welcomed, go into its streets and say, "Even the dust of your town that sticks to our feet we wipe off against you. Yet be sure of this: The kingdom of God is near." (Luke 10:8–11)

What did Jesus and his disciples experience? The poor, the sick, and the outcast gave an extraordinary reception to their proclamation of the kingdom. Whether in Galilee or in Judea, crowds gathered as soon as word spread that Jesus was coming. But the leaders were not converted. And their resistance jeopardized the success of Jesus' messianic mission. "Woe to you, Korazin! Woe to you, Bethsaida! For if the miracles that were performed in you had been performed in Tyre and Sidon, they would have repented long ago…" Even Capernaum – the center of the Messiah's activities—had slipped out of his grasp. "And you, Capernaum, will you be lifted up to the skies? No, you will go down to the depths…I tell you, it will be more bearable on that day for Sodom than for that town" (Luke 10:12–15).

On "the day of judgment" Tyre, Sidon, Sodom, and with them Korazin, Bethsaida, Capernaum, and Jerusalem, will appear before God. The pagan cities will be treated with less rigor than the Jewish ones that witnessed the miracles of the Messiah and had more opportunities to acclaim him as king. Those cities specifically condemned will cease to exist, whereas others, the forgiven, regenerated, and restored ones, will open their doors to the Messiah. "I tell you," Jesus said to Jerusalem, "you will not see me again until you say, 'Blessed is he who comes in the name of the Lord.'"[6]

King of the Jews

Our discussion about "power" in Israel and about the hope for a collective conversion of its cities can be enlarged by an examination of Jesus' messianic titles—King of the Jews, Son of David, Son of Man, Son of God, and Christ.

These titles disappear from Paul's vocabulary; he retains only the two terms "Son" and "Christ." This, however, actually underscores the primitive character—closer to historical Judaism—of the messianic titles used in the synoptic Gospels. The Greek or the Roman to whom Paul was preaching would not have understood these titles. There was no historical context to give them meaning. On the other hand, it is obvious that the Gospel writers did not doubt that Jesus was the King of the Jews, the Messiah announced by the prophets.

But the Jews, in particular the Pharisees, understood these titles and seem to have used them indiscriminately, never doubting Jesus' royal claims. On one point, however, Jesus disappointed their messianic expectations. Whereas they were awaiting a triumphant messianic king who would overcome his enemies by armed might, Jesus—while also preparing himself for a brilliant victory—would go the way of humiliation and voluntary sacrifice, like the "suffering servant" announced by Isaiah (Isa. 53). The Son of Man, the very one who was to come on the clouds of heaven, did not even have a stone on which to lay his head. Rejected by his own people, abandoned by his disciples, he was prepared to be handed over to the authorities and be crucified.[7] Regardless, in Jesus' mind the humiliated Messiah and the triumphant Messiah were one and the same. Were this not true, several of his well-known parables would lose all meaning.

For example, how should we understand the parable of the marriage feast (Matt. 22:1–14)? Jesus described himself as the son of a king (God), for whom his father is giving a banquet. The Jewish people respond to the invitation with indifference, insults, and violence toward the messengers. The affront to the king and his son is humiliating, but the invitation still stands. The wedding still takes place, but the guests come from the crossroads and along the hedges (from among the pagans). The feast honoring the king's son will take place no matter what happens, with or without the Jews.

Or take the teaching of the great judgment (Matt. 25:31ff.), which defines even more clearly Jesus' royal character. Who is the Son of Man,[8] coming in his glory with all his angels and sitting on his glorious throne, if not Jesus himself who at present is hungry, thirsty, naked, ill, a stranger in prison? It is impossible to give this parable any meaning if one claims, as some exegetes do, that Jesus did not see himself as the Son of Man who was to come in glory. Again, the humble Messiah and the victorious Messiah are one and the same.

This interpretation of these parables is confirmed by the account of Jesus' double trial, before Pilate and before the Sanhedrin. Unquestionably, both trials had a political character. The elders of the people, the chief priests, and the scribes knew that Pilate would refuse to get involved in theological quarrels between various Jewish sects. So they formulated a politically charged accusation against Jesus: "We have found this man subverting our nation. He opposes payment of taxes to Caesar and claims to be Christ, a king" (Luke 23:1–3). When Pilate heard this accusation, he asked Jesus a political question, "Are you the king of the Jews?" Jesus answered him unambiguously by assuming the title, King of the Jews: "Yes, it is as you say."[9]

Pilate may have doubted that Jesus' revolution could present any danger to the order of his province, but he had no doubts about the political demands of a man who so clearly identified himself to be the king of the Jews. So Pilate classified Jesus with the Zealots and with messianic pretenders who from time to time laid claim to the throne of Israel. Jesus' royal claims were obvious to the Romans. That is why the cohort mocked him. They covered him with a royal robe, set a grotesque crown of thorns on his head, placed a ridiculous scepter in his hand and kneeled before him, simulating an audience at a king's court, saying, "Hail, king of the Jews!" (Matt. 27:27–31). Indeed, if one wanted to remove Jesus' royal claims, it would be necessary to rewrite the Gospels!

The Sanhedrin itself was politically motivated in arresting Jesus. During the meeting that finalized Jesus' death, the chief priests and the Pharisees openly admitted, "If we let him go on like this, everyone will believe in him, and then the Romans will come and take away both our temple and our nation" (John 11:47–48).[10] Thus they condemned Jesus on the basis of political rationale. In their view Jesus' popularity was endangering both their authority and influence and the existence of the nation. Jesus had entered Jerusalem as a pretender to the royal throne. His imposture had to be unmasked.[11]

Consequently, the high priest questioned Jesus in no ambiguous terms, "I charge you under oath by the living God: Tell us if you are the Christ, the Son of God" (Matt. 26:63). And Jesus answered, as he did to Pilate, "Yes, it is as you say," and added, "But I say to all of you: In the future you will see the Son of Man sitting at the right hand of the Mighty One and coming on the clouds of heaven" (Matt. 26:63–64).

What did Jesus mean by "Son of Man"? In Daniel, the "son of man, coming with the clouds of heaven" is a mythical character, designated in particular as a king of Israel who will succeed a dynasty of tyrants. Following are the words of Daniel's prophecy that inspired Jesus' response to the high priest:

> As I looked, thrones were set in place, and the Ancient of Days took his seat…The court was seated, and the books were opened. Then I continued to watch because of the boastful words the horn was speaking. I kept looking until the beast was slain and its body destroyed and thrown into the blazing fire. (The other beasts had been stripped of their authority,[12] but were allowed to live for a period of time.)
>
> In my vision at night I looked, and there before me was one like a son of man, coming with the clouds of heaven. He approached the Ancient of Days and was led into his presence. He was given authority, glory and sovereign power; all peoples, nations and men of every language worshipped him. His dominion is an everlasting dominion that will not pass away, and his kingdom is one that will never be destroyed…
>
> The four great beasts are four kingdoms that will rise from the earth. But the saints of the Most High will receive the kingdom and will possess it forever—yes, for ever and ever. (Daniel 7:9–18)

By presenting himself as the Son of Man, Jesus was laying claim to the throne of Israel, a claim as unequivocal as the question put to Jesus by the high priest. In effect, the judiciary problem facing the Sanhedrin was two-sided. The first aspect was religious. Was this Jesus really the Son of God as he claimed? The other was political. Was Jesus telling the truth when he said he was the king of Israel announced by Daniel and the prophets?

When Jesus answered his interrogators in the affirmative, the Sanhedrin thought he was lying. The high priest tore his garments and cried out, "Why do we need any more witnesses?…You have heard the blasphemy. What do you think?" They answered, "He is worthy of death." For the Law stated, "Anyone who blasphemes the name of the Lord must be put to death. The entire assembly must stone him" (Lev. 24:16). So Jesus was condemned to death. He was not only politically dangerous, but had blasphemed by claiming the title of Messiah, King of Israel.[13]

Followers of King Jesus

Having outlined the political role Jesus had assigned to himself, we can now show the role his disciples were to play under his reign.

Up to the end of his earthly life Jesus assumed, if not insisted on, a continuity with Israel. True, there would be only a remnant, a handful of disciples who, despite their betrayal, would take part in the advancement of Jesus' reign, even after his crucifixion.

Near the time of his departure, Jesus addressed his twelve disciples and declared, "You are those who have stood by me in my trials. And I confer on you a kingdom, just as my Father conferred one on me" (Luke 22:28–29). It is difficult to see the meaning of such a bequest if the kingdom to which Jesus referred was purely celestial. In Jesus' mind the kingdom was both earthly and heavenly, present and future.[14] He leaves his disciples on earth to continue working for his kingdom.

But of what does this work consist? What did Jesus mean when he told his disciples they would "judge the twelve tribes of Israel"?

First, let us recall the role played by the "judges" in ancient Israel. A judge was not only in charge of administering justice, but also responsible for governing the people under God's direct authority. When Jesus told his disciples they would judge the twelve tribes of Israel, he was not necessarily referring to the last judgment. Rather, he was announcing that his apostles would act as governors or rulers of a new Israel. These were responsibilities he himself had inherited from God, his Father.

The parable of the ten minas confirms this. It reads as follows:

A man of noble birth went to a distant country to have himself appointed king and then to return. So he called ten of his servants and gave them ten minas [about three months' wages]. "Put this money to work," he said, "until I come back."

But his subjects hated him and sent a delegation after him to say, "We don't want this man to be our king."

He was made king, however, and returned home. Then he sent for the servants to whom he had given the money, in order to find out what they had gained with it.

The first one came and said, "Sir, your mina has earned ten more."

"Well done, my good servant!" his master replied. "Because you have been trustworthy in a very small matter, take charge of ten cities."

The second came and said, "Sir, your mina has earned five more."

His master answered, "You take charge of five cities."

Then another servant came and said, "Sir, here is your mina; I have kept it laid away in a piece of cloth. I was afraid of you, because you are a hard man. You take out what you did not put in and reap what you did not sow."

His master replied, "I will judge you by your own words, you wicked servant! You knew, did you, that I am a hard man...Why then didn't you put my money on deposit, so that when I came back, I could have collected it with interest?"

Then he said to those standing by, "Take his mina away from him and give it to the one who has ten minas."

"Sir," they said, "he already has ten!"

He replied, "I tell you that to everyone who has, more will be given, but as for the one who has nothing, even what he has will be taken away. But those enemies of mine who did not want me to be king over them—bring them here and kill them in front of me." (Luke 19:12–27)

A similar judgment is spoken in the parable of the tenants. When the people heard it they exclaimed, "May this never be!" Jesus looked directly at them and asked, "Then what is the meaning of that which is written: 'The stone the builders rejected has become the capstone'? Everyone who falls on that stone will be broken to pieces, but he on whom it falls will be crushed" (Luke 20:17–18). At this, the teachers of the law and the chief priests looked for a way to arrest Jesus. They knew that he had directed this parable against them.

One wonders whether Jesus' words are parables at all, especially since the people had heard his messianic call and were convinced that the kingdom of God was about to appear. Jesus speaks with the intention of making his position clear, and he plainly tells his disciples that they will soon be called upon to govern the cities of Israel. Herein lies the emphasis of the parable.

Despite Jesus' grim predictions about the outcome of his journey to Jerusalem, he had no doubt about the ultimate success of his campaign. He had chosen and drawn disciples around him, and they would lead and govern a new Israel. But before this would happen, they would have to face a period of trial. Jesus knew that the kingdom would have to wait, and he exhorted his disciples not to be deceived, but to persevere throughout their trials.

Jesus explained all this by recalling one of the memories of his youth. When Jesus was a child, Archelaus, one of Herod's sons, who was to succeed his father as one of the kings of the Herodian dynasty, had become very unpopular among the inhabitants of Jerusalem. He therefore traveled to Rome in order to receive the confirmation of his kingship from Emperor Augustus. But a Jewish delegation of his opponents caught up with him in Rome, and Augustus granted them Archelaus's deposition instead.[15]

In effect, Jesus was telling the crowd, "The authorities in Jerusalem do not want me for their king. I must appear before

God, the supreme sovereign, to receive my investiture from him and then I will come back. Do not think that what happened to Archelaus will also happen to me. The objections the Jewish authorities present before God's throne against my rule will not stand. I will surely return soon, invested with power and authority. Then a twofold judgment will take place: first, a judgment against my enemies, those who do not want me to rule over them, and second, a judgment over my disciples, who have administered my kingdom during my absence. The careless, doubting ones will be excluded from my kingdom, while the active, faithful ones will govern with me."

More could be said about this parable, but one further observation should be noted. The delay God grants grows out of his unbelievable patience. In the parable of the vineyard, God's patience comes to an end and punishment follows. In the parable of the minas, however, God still has pity on Israel and the punishment is put off until the day the king will return, invested with supreme authority.

Now we can understand Jesus' frame of reference as he went to Jerusalem mounted on a donkey to be acclaimed king. He was accomplishing a historical act. He was passing a new milestone on the way to the reestablishment of the kingdom of Israel and the founding of God's reign. As the crowd acclaimed him king, and as he accepted the cries of the children in the temple, "Hosanna to the Son of David," Jesus did not lament the tragic events awaiting him. Instead he cried over Jerusalem, over the cities of Israel, over the men, women, and children he had tried to bring together under the leadership of those who had the authority, all of whom had rejected him and his rulership.

In emphasizing Jesus' universal redemptive significance, Christian theology has tended to isolate Jesus from any concrete social or political context. As Son of God and Son of Man, Jesus is thus understood as having entered some invisible kingdom after all his disciples either denied or betrayed him. There is a complete break between the old Israel, ending at the cross, and the new Israel, the church, that grows out of the resurrection and the coming of the Spirit at Pentecost.

A break indeed occurred, but not in the historical or political nature of God's kingdom. Jesus came to bring a revolution, one that would impact every sphere of existence, including social and power relations. His message of repentance called for an about-face on the part of both individuals and entire cities. He did not want to reform political structures but wanted everything to come under God's rulership.

CHAPTER FIVE

Ethics of the Revolution

The question now arises as to what extent the new Israel – the church – can practice the jubilean mandate. In this chapter we will make only a summary exploration, which will be developed later on.

How shall we bridge the gap between Jesus' revolution and today's Christianity? To understand the significance of the Jubilee – "a Sabbath of sabbatical years" – that Jesus envisioned, we must first dig deeper into the meaning of the Sabbath itself. For herein lies the bridge we are looking for. Creation, God's kingdom, the Sabbath, and the Jubilee are so thoroughly intertwined in Jesus' understanding that both Israel's destiny and the earth's redemption are described in the New Testament as a state of holy rest.

The Final Sabbath

It is clear in the Old Testament that the Sabbath has eschatological significance (Exodus 20). It announces God's rest, the completion of his work in final perfection.

The Sabbath also has redemptive significance. In Deuteronomy 5 it is a reminder of the exodus from Egypt: "Remember that you were slaves in Egypt…Therefore the Lord your God has commanded you to observe the Sabbath day." The liberation of God's people out of Egypt was, in fact, announcing the supreme liberation at the end of history. God's people were to commemorate it and proclaim it by resting and by granting rest to the stranger, to the slaves, and even to the cattle. From the very beginning, the Sabbath concerned itself primarily with the human condition. The humanitarian concerns that inspired Jesus and his healing work already fill the pages of Deuteronomy: "On that day you shall not do any work, neither you, nor your son or daughter, nor your manservant or maidservant, nor your ox, your donkey or any of your animals, nor the alien within your gates, *so that your manservant and maidservant may rest, as you do"* (italics mine).

As we have already seen, the freeing of slaves during the sabbatical year was inspired by a similar consideration. God's liberation is the basis of the Sabbath. Even the ban on taking the garments of a sojourner, an orphan, or a widow as a pledge, or the requirement to leave what remains after harvest for the fatherless and widows, is justified on this basis: "Remember that you were slaves in Egypt and the Lord your God redeemed you from there. That is why I command you to do this" (Deut. 24:18).

According to Isaiah, God's essential work is the redemption of his people, which God himself accomplishes by means of his *goel,* the Messiah. When Jesus healed on the Sabbath he was accomplishing God's original purpose. Jesus' mission as well as his attitude toward the Sabbath is defined by the eschatological day of God's liberating rest. Far from wanting to abolish the Sabbath, Jesus wanted to restore it to its full significance. The Sabbath was not to be a day of servitude, but rather the premonitory sign of the supreme liberation God is accomplishing for his people and for the whole of creation.[1]

This supreme Sabbath is vividly portrayed in the latter part of Isaiah, probably written after the return from exile. Once back in their own land, the Jews had tried to establish a theocracy. They had restored the Sabbath to its place. Messianic hopes were intense: "Arise, shine, for your light has come, and the glory of the Lord rises upon you...Nations will come to your light and kings to the brightness of your dawn...The sun will no more be your light by day, nor will the brightness of the moon shine on you, for the Lord will be your everlasting light, and your God will be your glory" (Isa. 60).

To prepare for this reign of light, the entire people were to put the Sabbath into practice:

> If you keep your feet from breaking the Sabbath...if you call the Sabbath a delight...then you will find your joy in the Lord, and I will cause you to ride on the heights of the land and to feast on the inheritance of your father Jacob...Yet on the day of your fasting, you do as you please and exploit all your workers. Your fasting ends in quarreling and strife, and in striking each other with wicked fists...Is not this the kind of fasting I have chosen: to loose the chains of injustice and untie the cords of the yoke, to set the oppressed free and break every yoke? Is it not to share your food with the hungry and to provide the poor wanderer with shelter—when you see the naked, to clothe him, and not to turn away from your own flesh and blood?[2] Then your light will break forth like the dawn, and your healing will quickly appear. (Isa. 58)

> And foreigners who bind themselves to the Lord to serve him... all who keep the Sabbath without desecrating it and who hold fast to my covenant—these I will bring to my holy mountain and give them joy in my house of prayer.[3] Their burnt offerings and sacrifices will be accepted on my altar; for my house will be called a house of prayer for all nations. (Isa. 56)

> "Behold, I will create new heavens and a new earth...As the new heavens and the new earth that I make will endure before me," declares the Lord, "so will your name and descendants endure. From one New Moon to another and from one Sabbath to another, all mankind will come and bow down before me," says the Lord. (Isa. 65–66)

The Early Christians

Since Jesus' vocation cannot be understood apart from the sabbatical verses in Isaiah, it is no wonder that the disciples were filled with messianic expectation. While on the road to Emmaus, they told the stranger (i.e., Jesus) accompanying them of that expectation and their disappointment concerning Jesus of Nazareth: "We had hoped that he was the one who was going to redeem Israel." And beginning with Moses and all the Prophets, the stranger explained to them what was said in all the Scriptures concerning himself (Luke 24:13–27).

Once back in Jerusalem, the Emmaus pilgrims were telling all this to the apostles when Jesus appeared among them. He said to them, "This is what I told you while I was still with you: Everything must be fulfilled that is written about me in the Law of Moses, the Prophets and the Psalms...This is what is written: The Christ will suffer and rise from the dead on the third day, and repentance and forgiveness of sins will be preached in his name to all nations, beginning at Jerusalem. You are witnesses of these things" (Luke 24:44–49).

It was in this atmosphere of expectation that the church in Jerusalem was formed. "Lord," the disciples asked Jesus before Pentecost, "are you at this time going to restore the kingdom to Israel?" And Jesus did not dissuade them from expecting the restoration of the kingdom. He merely warned them, as he did in Jericho on the eve of his trip to Jerusalem, that "it is not for you to know the times or dates the Father has set by his own authority" (Acts 1:6–7).

It was natural, therefore, for Peter, in his speech to the people after healing a lame man, to link the Jubilee with God's final restoration, the final Sabbath. He, like Jesus, spells out a perfectly clear eschatological program: "Repent, then, and turn to God, so that your sins may be wiped out, that times of refreshing may come from the Lord, and that he may send the Christ, who has been appointed for you—even Jesus. He must remain in heaven until the time comes for God to restore everything, as he promised long ago through his holy prophets. For Moses said, 'The Lord your God will raise up for you a prophet like me from among your own people; you must listen to everything he tells you'" (Acts 3:19–22).

For the first Christians the resurrection, Pentecost, and the expectation that all things would be restored required an immediate application of Moses' sabbatical teachings, as interpreted by Jesus. The Jubilee was a part of these teachings, and they put it into practice:

> All the believers were together and had everything in common. Selling their possessions and goods, they gave to anyone as he had need…All the believers were one in heart and mind. No one claimed that any of his possessions was his own, but they shared everything they had…There were no needy persons among them. From time to time those who owned lands or houses sold them, brought the money from the sales and put it at the apostles' feet, and it was distributed to anyone as he had need. (Acts 2:44–45, 4:32–35)

Much debate has centered on the "impossible communism" of the early church in Jerusalem. Some commentators think the idyllic description in Acts is exaggerated. They underscore the fact that the text mentions only one concrete example of land sharing, that of Joseph, called Barnabas, who sold a field. If all those who owned land sold it, why did the author think it necessary to emphasize Barnabas's example? Others recognize the communism of the early church, but claim that it was short-lived. They say it belonged to the "interim ethics"[4] Jesus preached, but became impossible to practice once the church recognized the length of the interval still separating it from the "restoration of all things."

Another school of thought argues that Jesus' Sermon on the Mount is to be understood solely in eschatological terms. The Beatitudes, for example, announce the coming deliverance that will in the future reward the poor, the mourners, the meek, the hungry, the merciful, the pure, the peacemakers, and the persecuted. These promises of a future kingdom, with its "kingdom ethics," are nevertheless in tension with today's world. Jesus articulates this future righteousness to help us measure the depth of our failure, to inspire us to repent, and to open the door of grace. We are not to apply Jesus' ethic literally. His commands form an absolute ideal by which to judge our relative good efforts.[5]

But this interpretation of Jesus' ethic is weak on several counts. First, it neglects the gospel's entire social message, which Jesus expressed so clearly. Second, it places each individual person within a series of "situations" where he or she alone must always resolve the tension between the absolute and the possible. This pushes a person into clashes of conscience he or she cannot always overcome, and undermines the important role of the church as a channel of God's commandments and forgiveness. Third, stripped of their social context, Jesus' commands become irrelevant. And once his commands have been undermined, we can no longer really see ourselves as the sinners we are, and God's grace becomes meaningless.[6]

Jesus did not intend to crush his people under the weight of an impossible absolute. Rather, he simply proclaimed a Jubilee – to use Peter's words, "times of refreshing" – announcing that the time had come "for God to restore everything."

With this, we are finally treading upon the solid ground of Jewish ethics. The Jubilee was a revolutionary year for an entire people and not only a set of norms for individuals or for a select few. Jesus' message is revolutionary, applicable to a society as well as to an individual. It is an ethic of possibility, adaptable[7] to each age, whenever the expectation of the kingdom becomes more intense under the influence of God's spirit.

This is what the members of early church experienced together.[8] Of course, the "times of refreshment" which followed Pentecost eventually passed. Then this Jubilee, characterized by the restitution of land and houses to the poor, by the sharing of possessions, and by the recovery of health for the sick, made way for a period of stabilization. People returned to their work, got married, and raised families.

Yet every time the gospel reached new groups, the proclamation of the Jubilee – the dawning of the final Sabbath – would ring out again. These Jubilees did not follow a pre-established calendar of septennial recurrences. Rather, as soon as Jews or Gentiles were touched by the apostles' message, they inaugurated their conversion with a Jubilee. One should read Paul's letters in this spirit. In particular, the beginning of each letter describes the extraordinary favors manifested in each city on the day when Jesus was recognized there as the Messiah. Chapters 8 and 9 of 2 Corinthians (written around A.D. 57, twenty-nine years after Pentecost) witness to the joy that filled the Macedonians, whose "extreme poverty welled up in rich generosity" in aiding the members of the church in Jerusalem.[9]

Dimming the Light

If the above picture appears too optimistic, what happened next will modify it. In A.D. 66 the Jews who had refused to accept the Messiah revolted against Rome. The Romans under Titus destroyed Jerusalem in A.D. 70, and the Jewish state ceased to exist. From then on the Mosaic Law lost its social and political thrust for the dispersed Jews. Indeed, in rabbinic literature the hopes for a reestablishment of Israel became vaguer and vaguer.

The Christians were subjected to an evolution similar to that of the Jews. Dispersed as they were throughout the Mediterranean countries, they adopted a minority ethic. It was out of the question for them to literally reestablish the sabbatical laws. They were busy remaining faithful under persecution, renouncing the impurities of the world, and keeping good relationships between members of the church. The messianic vision of a kingdom of God, which would begin in Israel and spread to the entire globe, slowly faded. It would probably be more exact to say that it turned into the expectation of heaven, meant for those who persevered in the present tribulations. Who could hope to reform the Roman Empire with the jubilean ideal? The church even came to think of the authority of Caesar and the *Pax Romana* as divine gifts.

Also, insofar as Israel did not become converted, and despite the hopes Paul formulated in Romans 11, the first Christians abandoned the ancient plan that set the conversion of Israel as the primary condition for the conversion of the nations. The church then specialized in the salvation of individuals. It recruited them one by one and exhorted them to remain faithful. The example of the martyrs brought about new conversions, but the church's hopes for a radically altered world shrank. The unconverted, both Jews and Gentiles, came to be considered definitively lost.

Three centuries later, the impossible happened. Rome was "converted" to Christianity and Emperor Constantine turned it into a state religion.[10] But the Roman state relied on Roman law and ignored Moses. Once in power, the church adopted Rome's social ethics as its own, while continuing to teach the minority ethic that had constituted its strength during persecution. The church forgot the Jubilee, which lingered on in the church's liturgy only as a vague nostalgia for forgotten messianic expectations.

But the spirit of the prophets never perished. Like the prophets of old, reformers shook up the church from century to century and attempted to bring it back to the original vision. These noble efforts sometimes resulted in the founding of a new religious order, sometimes in the creation of a new reforming movement, often oriented toward the jubilean practice of shared possessions.[11] Over the centuries the jubilee light dimmed but did not go out.

The Jubilee Extended

Despite the church's failure to consistently apply Jesus' jubilean revolution, several of its norms are still applicable for our day. First, social and political revolutions are not in principle contrary to the Old Testament or to the gospel. Their periodic recurrence indicates that they may be necessary in restoring God's justice in an otherwise deteriorating social order.

Second, we must condemn privileged social classes or races who refuse, in the name of Christ or faith, to do justice, or who violently repress revolutionary movements. It was because they refused the Jubilee that the Jewish leaders crucified the Christ and hastened Jerusalem's catastrophic end. Although the murderous violence of some revolutions is certainly contrary to the gospel, revolution itself cannot be condemned when it is prompted by a desire for justice or by desperation. Furthermore, it is wrong to believe that Christians should not worry about social matters. The divorce between individual ethics and social practices is found neither in the gospel nor in Judaism. Such a fissure is but a compromise on the church's part, a corruption rooted in a false alliance with a pagan society whose laws do not arise from biblical revelation.

Third, whenever the spirit of God speaks to the church it is a call to repentance–a transformation of policy and habits both in individuals and in the whole. Individual conversion and social repentance cannot be dissociated. The gospel ethic is one of renewal, for in the Old Testament tradition Jubilees were nothing less than religious awakenings. Any effort to limit an awakening by preventing it from bearing fruit on the social and political levels will cause it to abort. We must not limit the full scope of God's power. "Jubilee awakenings" will bring new life to individuals, affect justice within the church, forge unity across denominational lines, and call society to practice God's righteousness.[12] In this way the church confirms the election it inherited from the people of Israel and from the Messiah.

Finally, in its proclamation of the Jubilee the church should not take the place of the state. The Jubilee does not bind people to laws; it frees them from servitude of any and every kind. It can only be conceived in a spirit of repentance and prayer. Modern states, even with their most beneficial social programs, have not inherited Israel's vocation. They can neither pray nor repent. So the church alone must be the embodiment of the Jubilee.

When the church experiences such a "time of refreshing," there is no longer irreconcilable tension between "the coming kingdom of God" with its so-called "absolute ethic" and "the world as it is" with its "relative necessities." And the Christian is no longer inwardly torn apart by conflicting duties to his Christian conscience and his membership in the state. The only tension that remains is that which separates the faithful church from the state.

The church that announces God's Jubilee, and puts it into practice as the Spirit blows, will show practical solutions to the problems of exploitation, oppression, inequality, and a whole host of other human evils. When this happens, the church will once again find its place in the world. Its members will grasp the full scope and implications of the gospel and apply them in the concrete reality of today's world. And it will take heed to the author of Hebrews when he exhorts, "There remains, then, a Sabbath-rest for the people of God...Let us, therefore, make every effort to enter that rest" (Heb. 4:9–11).

PART II

Jesus and His Contemporaries

CHAPTER SIX

Precursors to Peace

Jesus proclaimed that the kingdom of God was at hand and that a great reversal was about to be unleashed. Mary understood right from the start: "He has performed mighty deeds with his arm; he has scattered those who are proud in their inmost thoughts. He has brought down rulers from their thrones, but has lifted up the humble. He has filled the hungry with good things, but has sent the rich away empty. He has helped his servant Israel, remembering to be merciful" (Luke 1:51–54).

But what kind of upheaval would this be? Would it demand a call to arms? Would it require the use of force? Did Jesus come to bring peace or a sword?

This next section will show how Jesus' revolution would bypass political intrigue and posturing; it would follow an altogether different path. He would fulfill God's plan of peace, of which the prophets had but a glimpse.

The Prophets

We cannot understand Jesus' way of peace apart from Israel's prophetic tradition. Elijah, who prophesied in Israel under Ahab (around 870 B.C.), was certainly the most ardent defender of sacred violence. To rid the Israelites of Canaanite idolatry, he did not hesitate to personally massacre 450 prophets of Baal, the rival of Yahweh. But this feat troubled him deeply. After having taken refuge in the desert, he did not find God's revelation in the earthquake or the fire, but in the "still small voice."

His disciple Elisha was also a man of extreme violence. He had two bears tear some children to pieces because they laughed at his baldness. Nevertheless, he advised the king of Israel toward moderation. When the king asked Elisha whether he should execute the Syrian prisoners he had captured, Elisha replied, "Do not kill them. Would you kill men you have captured with your own sword or bow? Set food and water before them so that they may eat and drink and then go back to their master." The king obeyed and sent the prisoners home. This act of mercy had providential consequences: the Syrians no longer raided the land of Israel (2 Kings 6:21–23).

Elisha died in 785 B.C. Thirty-five years later, Amos, the first prophet-writer, ushered in the vision of a peaceable Hebrew nationalism. Amos was certainly not a sentimental man, nor was he thinking of weakening Israel's virility. His prophecies against the enemies of the Jews are extremely violent, but the ones he pronounced against his own people are more so. He blamed his fellow Israelites for their own sufferings, which he saw as chastisements sent by God for their crimes of injustice. Amos understood that sacred violence, necessary to reestablish God's justice, applied equally to the friends as well as to the enemies of Yahweh. Yahweh could no longer be a national god. He was the universal judge of all the nations.[1]

This trend towards universal justice was accentuated with the prophets to follow. The prophet Hosea compared Israel to a woman who deceived her husband by "committing adultery" with foreign gods. Her infidelity was chastised by means of the Assyrians, but God continued to love.

Isaiah dissuaded Hezekiah, king of Judah, from making an alliance with Egypt. In 721 B.C., the Assyrians had taken Samaria, the capital of the Northern Kingdom, and carried away its inhabitants. Jerusalem, the capital of the small Southern Kingdom, seemed doomed to the same fate. The Jews wavered between profound discouragement and the superficial optimism of reliance on Egypt. But Isaiah reminded them to trust God alone. As the tremendous armies of Sennacherib, king of the Assyrians, were moving in on the capital, deliverance came. A plague struck the Assyrians' camp, and they withdrew.

This same Isaiah left us a series of portraits of the "Servant of the Lord." The Servant of the Lord was the Jewish people, a people called to be a light to the nations and to establish justice on earth. God's Servant would find his security nowhere but in God, for God alone was in charge of his protection. Isaiah was already sketching a new method of national defense, so to speak, tied to Israel's acceptance of its particular vocation as Servant of the Lord.

Jeremiah, the sorrowing prophet who witnessed Jerusalem's destruction, followed in Isaiah's footsteps. The generals of Nebuchadnezzar, king of Chaldea, laid siege to Jerusalem, but it refused to capitulate. Jeremiah disapproved of military resistance and advised the people to have faith in God alone. He was thrown into jail for attempting to escape the besieged city. From his dungeon cell, he continued to cry out even at the risk of his life, "This is what the Lord says: 'Whoever stays in this city will die by the sword...but whoever goes over to the Babylonians will live...This city will certainly be handed over to the army of the king of Babylon, who will capture it" (Jer. 38:2–3). The people did not listen to him and the divine warning was realized. Jerusalem was taken and destroyed in 587 B.C. and its people carried off to Babylon.

The Jews no longer had a problem of national defense during the exile; they were, of course, captives and powerless. It was at this time that the "prophet of the exile," usually called the second Isaiah, witnessed the unjust suffering endured by the exiled and completed the portrait of the Servant of the Lord. "Here is my servant, whom I uphold, my chosen one in whom I delight; I will put my Spirit on him and he will bring justice to the nations," he cried. "He will not falter or be discouraged till he establishes justice on earth." But, he noted, he will establish this justice without breaking a bruised reed or quenching a dimly burning wick (Isa. 42:1–4).

Certainly, the people would be judged for their disobedience and crimes, but a remnant was to survive. Jerusalem would be restored. The sufferings of the Lord's servant would redeem the sins of many.

From this came the idea of the *goel* of Israel, of Yahweh participating with his people in a much wider redemptive act, intended for the entire human race. When God redeems the guilty, it is not because he fails to see the power of evil or to look at the world as it is. Redemption does not eliminate divine violence, but rather redirects it from the head of God's enemy to the Lord's servant, who is called to suffer on behalf of the guilty. Evil is overcome by redemptive love. God the avenger of his oppressed people liberates them by dying for them.[2]

National Resistance

In addition to Israel's prophetic tradition, Jesus inherited a history of national resistance. In fact, from the exile until Jesus' time, Israel's history was one long struggle for the acceptance or rejection of this grand and terrible vocation of Servant of the Lord.[3] In 538 B.C., one of Cyrus's edicts had brought the Jews back to Palestine. The temple had been rebuilt and the people were filled with great hopes. But the ideal theocracy imagined by Ezekiel was not about to become a reality. Subjected to the Persians from

538 to 333 B.C., to the Greeks under Alexander the Great, then to the Ptolemys of Egypt, and finally to the Seleucids of Syria from 197 B.C. on, Israel became entrenched in religious legalism. Ritual observance replaced living faith. Courage was not lacking, but the powerful nonviolent visions of the prophets had vanished.

Moreover, a new ideology began to supersede the biblical faith. The tolerant Greek civilization was slowly invading Asia. Even the high priests in Jerusalem were becoming hellenized. Under the rule of the Seleucids of Syria, the Jews gradually adopted their customs. In 175 B.C., Jason, the father of the high priest Onias, became the advocate of the new ideas in Jerusalem.

Hellenization was increasing at a steady pace when finally a backlash erupted. Antiochus Epiphanes, king of Syria, abolished Jewish worship and erected a statue of Zeus in the temple of Jerusalem. On the 24th of Chislev, 167 B.C., a pagan sacrifice defiled the holy place. (This was later called the "abomination of the desolation." Jesus said a recurrence of such a sacrilege after his death would be a sign that the end was near.) For fear of persecution, the majority of the Jews accepted the new cult. Only one priest, Mattathias, filled with righteous anger, left Jerusalem and went to Modin in order to remain faithful to the Law of Moses. His five sons followed him. The Hasidaeans, a group of puritans that preceded the Pharisees, also joined them. Quite a number of people concerned with justice and holiness followed Mattathias's example and fled to the desert. Royal troops pursued and reached them.

Mattathias was not in principle against violence; he had personally cut the throat of a Jew who had sacrificed to idols. In its first stage, however, his resistance was passive. A group of the faithful refused to retaliate rather than fight their aggressors on the Sabbath. "Let us all die in our innocence," they said. "Heaven and earth testify for us that you are killing us unjustly." The enemy attacked them on the Sabbath. They allowed themselves to be massacred without resisting, remaining faithful to the law that forbade them to fight on the Sabbath.

After hearing about this massacre, however, Mattathias chose to use violence: "If we all do as our brethren have done and refuse to fight for our lives and our customs, our enemies will quickly destroy us from the earth." He therefore called the Jews to arms and began a war of liberation, which his sons would end victoriously.[4]

At Mattathias's death, his son Judas, nicknamed Maccabee ("the hammer"), mercilessly struck their enemies. In 164 B.C. the temple was purified. In 160 B.C. Jonathan succeeded his brother Judas, who had been killed at war. In 143 B.C. the third brother, Simon, became the high priest and ethnarch of Palestine. When the Maccabees had regained Jewish national independence, they took the titles of high priest and king. But unfortunately the Maccabees, or Hasmonaeans, were unable to free themselves from the violence they had used to obtain power. In order to reestablish the ancient boundaries of David's kingdom, they warred with their neighbors and took Perea, Samaria, Idumea, and Philistia. Approximately one century later, their conflict-ridden dynasty crumpled before foreign usurpers, the Herods.

The Hasidaeans, who had supported Mattathias, became a political party, the Pharisees, champions of strict ritual observances. They entered the struggle for power. Persecuted under Alexander Janneus, they triumphed under his daughter Alexandra.

Several pretenders to the throne hastened the decline of the Hasmonaeans. In 65 B.C., Hyrcan, supported by a "mayor of the palace," Antipater the Idumean, contended with his younger brother Aristobulus, who entrenched himself in Jerusalem.

Finally the Romans came onto the scene. Pompey took the side of Hyrcan in 63 B.C. and laid siege to Jerusalem. After three months, his soldiers made a breach in the wall, stormed and took the city. The victorious Roman general then entered the "holy of holies" with his forces, scandalizing the Jews. But he was wiser than Antiochus Epiphanes a century earlier. He ordered the temple to be purified and the traditional sacrifices offered. Hyrcan retained the pontificate, but his role was reduced to that of ethnarch while his minister Antipater was given the Greek title of *epitropos* (equivalent to the Latin "procurator") by Pompey.

The success for Antipater's family began that day. Antipater was not a Jew. He was an Idumean, or Edomite. Neither he nor his son Herod had any right to the throne of Israel. However, by associating themselves with the changing fortunes of the Roman political figures who rivaled for the dictatorship (Pompey, Caesar, Anthony, and finally Octavius, the future Augustus), the Herods managed to obtain royal power from them. The trickery Antipater and Herod the Great employed to attain their ends (for example, deserting the camp of a conquered general in order to offer service to the conqueror) help explain the Jews' repulsion for this dynasty of usurpers.

But Herod the Great was not lacking in genius; in fact, he was a man of powerful intellect. As the last of the Hasmonaeans, Antigonus, was besieging him in Jerusalem, Herod managed to escape to Rome and have Anthony declare him king of Judea. He was solemnly crowned in 39 B.C., but then had to re-conquer his kingdom by force. In 37 B.C. he took Jerusalem and reinstated the cult. Eighteen years later he began the construction of a magnificent temple, which became famous throughout the world and drew the admiration of Jesus' disciples.

Herod reigned for thirty-three years, until 4 B.C. Unfortunately, history leaves a rather biased picture of him. The first part of his reign was actually very prosperous. A great admirer of Greek customs, he had an amphitheater built outside Jerusalem's gates, as well as a theater and a magnificent palace for himself within the city. During a famine, he ordered food distribution to the poor. But his family was busy plotting against him. Herod became morbidly jealous; he executed, one after another, his father-in-law, his mother-in-law, one of his ten wives, and three of his daughters. The monstrous cruelties that marked the end of his reign erased in the people's minds any recollection of the positive aspects of his character. His death was acclaimed as a deliverance.

Jesus was born during Herod the Great's reign. He was two or three years old when Herod died, after his failed attempt to kill Jesus with the children of Bethlehem. In the period following Herod's death, one pseudo-messiah after another attempted to seize political power. Jesus often referred to these tragic events of his childhood. They would help to define his mission and demarcate his way from all the others.

CHAPTER SEVEN

Crises in Palestine

W e now come to the social and political setting in which Jesus
found himself. In Jesus' day Palestine was a hotbed of conflict. It was indeed one of the most violent and oppressive epochs
in Jewish history, with the cauldron of agitation reaching its apex
in the destruction of Jerusalem. Jesus' message of Jubilee would
not likely be received as a benign word of hope. The climate was
thick with unrest. Any proclamation risked inciting revolution.

Political Unrest

Herod the Great's death in 4 B.C. caused a serious succession of
crises. The king's will divided the kingdom among his three sons.
Philip received the land beyond the Jordan. Archelaus inherited
Judea, Idumea, and Samaria, with the title of king; and Herod,
called Antipas, received Galilee and Perea.

When Jesus crossed the Sea of Galilee, he would go into Philip's
territory. Philip reigned there peacefully until A.D. 34 without
problems. In Judea, however, Archelaus's reign would last only
ten years and would be filled with disturbances. For instance,
after several attempts to appease the people, he executed three
thousand Jews to suppress an insurrection. His brothers contested

the validity of their father's will, which had made Archelaus king while they were only tetrarchs. Archelaus went to Rome as early as A.D. 4 to petition Augustus for royal investiture, which the emperor granted him. But Jewish delegations hostile to the king repeatedly went to Rome and finally obtained his deposition. He was exiled to Vienne in Gaul in A.D. 6.[1]

By getting rid of Archelaus, the Jews had hoped to regain their independence. But as it turned out, the exact opposite happened. Augustus turned Judea and Samaria into Roman provinces and incorporated them with Syria, which at that time was under the authority of an imperial legate. He governed Judea by means of a procurator residing at Caesarea on the coast. We know the names of the procurators of Judea: Coponius, Valerius Gratus, Pontius Pilate (from A.D. 26 to 36), and Marcellus, who succeeded each other until A.D. 37. After Marcellus, from A.D. 37 to 44, the Jewish kingdom was temporarily reunited under a grandson of Herod the Great, Agrippa I. Having spent his childhood in Rome, Agrippa had become a good friend of Caligula, who became emperor in A.D. 37.

At Agrippa's death, Judea again became a procuratorial province. One procurator succeeded another quite rapidly, until the great revolt of A.D. 66 broke out, which caused the destruction of Jerusalem.

In Galilee, Herod Antipas, a contemporary of Jesus, is closely tied to the gospel story. In honor of Tiberius, he had built a city on the Sea of Galilee, which he named Tiberias. He forced settlers to come and live there and turned it into his capital. However, it was built on a cemetery, which was considered a sacrilege by pious Jews. They would not set foot in it.

Antipas divorced his first wife, daughter of Aretas, king of Arabia, and married Herodias, the wife of one of his numerous brothers. This insult to his first wife's father set off a war, which

Antipas eventually lost. John the Baptist, who was then preaching near the Jordan, had enough courage to reproach the king for a marriage he considered incestuous. The Gospel narrative of Herodias' vengeance and of John the Baptist's death is well known (Matt. 14:1–12; Mark 6:16–29). According to the historian Flavius Josephus, Antipas had John the Baptist executed because his preaching endangered the throne.[2] It was a threat to the social and political order.

In A.D. 37, at the time of the accession of Agrippa I to the throne of Judea, the ambitious Herodias became infuriated after seeing Agrippa receive a higher title than her husband and incited her husband to also go to Rome in order to obtain the title of king. Unhappily for Antipas, Caligula decided to send him into exile in Lugdunum in Spain.

Pilate, the sixth procurator, also came to a sad end. (A later chapter will describe the troubles during his term of office.) Having been denounced before the legate of Syria, he was removed from office in A.D. 36 and sent to Rome to justify himself. He was most likely exiled, perhaps to Gaul.

Oppression

The political instability of Palestine was exacerbated by the way the Romans administered it. First, the Roman procurator was a minor official, dependent on the legates. Each procurator had only a small number of troops, so when disturbances occurred in Judea, the procurator had to call upon the legate. In short, Rome did not always have immediate or easy means to squelch social unrest.

In some respects, the political regime Rome imposed upon its Galilean protectorate and Judean province was not as harsh as it could have been. In theory Rome respected the religion of a conquered people. Thus, religious services took place as usual at the temple in Jerusalem. A sacrifice to Yahweh was offered daily in the name of the emperor. The Roman cohort, who resided in the Antonia tower to the north of the temple, was even responsible for guarding the sacerdotal garb. This is because the Jews often quarreled over the succession of the high priest. Although the high priest was no longer king, he continued to judge the people according to the Law of Moses, along with the Sanhedrin. Though the Romans limited the Sanhedrin's power—in particular, the right to pronounce and carry out capital punishment—a measure of religious freedom was granted to the Jews. Roman garrisons occupied the land, but except for periods of mutiny, they seem rarely to have had contact with the Jews themselves.

At the time of Herod's accession to the throne, Palestine was still one of the richest countries along the eastern Mediterranean. Herod showered not only Jerusalem but all of Palestine with his generosity. He was a construction maniac. He erected the Herodium, his fabulous fortress and retreat near Bethlehem. The cities of Antipatris, Phasaelis Sebaste, and Caesarea were completely rebuilt, as well as the old Tower of Strato.

Despite certain provisions or privileges, Palestine remained one of the most restless provinces in the empire.[3] With such expensive building projects, for example, Herod overburdened the people with taxes. Galilee was hit the hardest because it was much richer agriculturally than the rocky hills of Judea. The Jews were already heavily taxed. First, they paid the temple tax, expected of everyone; then the first-fruits and the tithe established by Moses to feed the sons of Levi. The Levites (approximately 20,000) took turns going to Jerusalem to serve in the temple, but the tithe rarely found its way to their homes. The high clergy appropriated it by force and thus grew richer. The low clergy often sided with the poor, which explains the priest Zechariah's style of piety and the family setting into which Jesus was born. Besides the tithe for the clergy, the Jews were supposed to pay another tithe for the poor, which was again often embezzled by the high clergy.

To these taxes prescribed by Jewish law, the Roman occupants added the tribute to Caesar. This unpopular tax included a land tax, a poll tax paid directly to the employees of the imperial treasury, and indirect taxes collected by the toll-gatherers. Palestine was subdivided into fiscal provinces whose revenue went to rich, often absentee landlords. By means of their agents, these individuals pressured the population into paying much more than the toll required by Rome. They had under their orders a large number of Jews whose offices kept an eye on the roads, bridges, borders, and ports. These tax collectors grew rich at the expense of the people, who, in turn, hated and rejected them.

According to some calculations, as much as 60 or 70 percent of a peasant's income eventually fell into the hands of various collectors and creditors.[4] Though loans with interest were in principle forbidden by the Jewish law, taxpayers unable to pay became victims of usurers, who would impose annual interest rates as high as 24 percent.[5] Because of heavy taxation small and middle-sized plots of land gradually disappeared, while properties owned by the temple and the imperial crown grew beyond proportion. The former owners had to work these lands as slaves.

Rarely, however, did a Jew ever remain a slave. His closest kinsman, his *goel*, usually sacrificed in order to pay his debts and set him free. Thus, in Jesus' time, everybody was familiar with the concept of ransom or "redemption." But the system of redemption had its limits. For instance, it did not affect the Jews who had been sentenced to the mines or the galleys following revolts, which had been harshly suppressed.

The mandate that ordered all fields to lie fallow during the seventh year also contributed to the impoverishment of the people. Driven to misery, many peasants abandoned their land

and joined bands of robbers that survived by pillage and lived in caves in the mountains.

It is difficult to determine whether these highway robbers were common criminals who simply attacked vulnerable peasants, or patriots with the dream of freeing Palestine from the Roman yoke. In any case, they were forced to find means of survival in the desert. Barabbas and the two robbers between whom Jesus was crucified were probably patriots of this type. This would explain the bitter irony of one of the men hanging beside Jesus: "Are you not the Christ? Save yourself and us!" (Luke 23:39). He was bitter toward Jesus for not having taken the leadership of the underground resistance.

Whatever the case may be, the rapid impoverishment of Palestine, and Galilee in particular, helps to explain the extraordinary response Jesus' jubilean proclamations found among the poor and the outcast. John the Baptist, who was baptizing at the Jordan River, had opened the way for the messianic revolution by proclaiming, "Prepare the way for the Lord, make straight paths for him. Every valley shall be filled in, every mountain and hill made low…The man with two tunics should share with him who has none, and the one who has food should do the same." He commanded the tax collectors, "Don't collect any more than you are required to" by the royal or Roman administration. He also exhorted Herod's soldiers and those of the occupation, who probably accompanied the tax collectors on their rounds, "Don't extort money and don't accuse people falsely – be content with your pay." John's message was a straightforward declaration of the imminence of a Jubilee, and the people waiting expectantly wondered if he might possibly be the Messiah (Luke 3:1–15).

Palestine was thus ripe for change. Its peace was at best tenuous, its hopes for liberation on the rise, and its myriad problems were only getting worse. Into this climate Jesus entered and proclaimed his message of liberation. How would it be received? Who would take it seriously and begin to live it out? Would it go the way of other social and political movements of the day, or would it find a different way to respond?

CHAPTER EIGHT

Resistance Movements

Palestine's political situation, its impoverishment, and the re-awakening of messianic hopes were important factors in the numerous revolts that shook Israel during Jesus' youth. The Jewish people were engaged in a life-and-death struggle for the survival of their nation and religion. In one way or another and to varying degrees, they resisted assimilation into the Greco-Roman world.

Tension

By Jesus' time the traditional religion of the Romans and the Greeks was already completely decadent. Educated people no longer considered their divinities to be symbols of one unique and unknowable God. Syncretism was overcoming the fanaticism of preceding centuries. Greek philosophy took upon itself the rec-onciliation of all the extremes. Philo of Alexandria, also known as the Jewish Plato, was attempting to harmonize Platonic phi-losophy and the Old Testament. And by writing his *Jewish Wars* and *Jewish Antiquities* in Greek, Josephus was bringing Judaism in line with the wisdom in fashion during the first century.

Emperor worship, through which Rome was to try to unify so many diverse religions and give a sense of duty to a crumbling world, was just beginning to form. Rome showed itself tolerant and granted to the peoples of the empire the right to practice their particular cult so long as they agreed to venerate Caesar. But in Rome itself the crowd practiced Oriental mysteries aimed at purifying the soul from sins. Among these, the cult of Mithra was a rival to nascent Christianity.

Judaism had also spread throughout the Mediterranean world where it had made many proselytes. In many cities, including Rome, Jews had formed sizable communities distinct from the rest of the population. People reproached them for their narrow fanaticism. Local custom prescribed that all inhabitants offer sacrifices to the local gods. But faithful Jews kept their own customs and refused to offer libations in honor of the gods. Consequently, they could not fully participate in the life of the community, bound as they were by their own law. The first Christians merely imitated them in this respect.

When friction occurred between the local authorities and the Jews, the latter usually appealed to Caesar on the basis of their rights. The emperor was wise enough to grant them privileges: the right to stop work and to hold gatherings on the Sabbath, the right to worship freely, and exemption from pagan ceremonies and certain taxes.

However, many Jews of respectable families had acquired Roman citizenship. This raised its own problems. Rome's subjects were not forced to serve in the army; they could enlist in the auxiliary troops if they so desired. But Roman citizens had both the privilege and the duty to serve in the legions. By becoming Roman citizens, the Jews were binding themselves to military service. However, the practice of the Sabbath and Jewish dietary restrictions could not be reconciled with Roman military life. This forced those Jews who were Roman citizens to plead for exemption from military service, which was eventually granted them by

Julius Caesar in 47 B.C. By the same edict, Caesar forbade Roman magistrates to raise auxiliary troops in Jewish territory and also exempted the Jews from the tribute during sabbatical years.[1]

This is probably why Jesus never had to tell his disciples to refuse military service. Even those who might have had Roman citizenship would have been exempted by the imperial edict. All pious Jews were conscientious objectors for ritual reasons, and Rome treated conscientious objectors with more tolerance than do some of our modern democracies.

Naturally, the Gentiles were often jealous of the Jews who formed privileged clans in the cities where they lived. There was rarely peaceful co-existence between Jews and their non-Jewish neighbors. And the exemption granted to Jewish "conscientious objectors" by Caesar was not always conceded by his successors. Under Tiberius, for example, the Jewish population of Rome was thrown out of the city. The consuls drafted four thousand men for military service. Josephus writes that they "sent them to the island of Sardinia and penalized a good many of them who refused to serve for fear of breaking the Jewish law."[2]

Revolt

The tension between Jews and Gentiles was most serious in Palestine itself, where the Jews constituted a majority. The slightest infringement upon their religious customs could and did trigger revolt.

It is hard to know which of the revolutionary leaders in Palestine actually claimed to be the Messiah. But keep in mind the intensity of messianic expectation and the sketchy details about the Messiah's attributes. The expected Messiah was to be a legitimate king of David's dynasty, both a military and religious leader, and a restorer of the purity of worship and of national independence. For the Jews, politics and religion were so entwined that anyone who tried to become king was practically claiming the title of Messiah.

During Jesus' early childhood, messianic agitation began to manifest itself publicly. Despite uncertainty about the dates, it seems that the census by Quirinius (Luke 2:2), the legate of Syria at that time, was the first event to set off an outbreak of resistance.[3] For pious Jews, the census raised a dilemma. Its sole aim was to set the tax base for the Romans, but it also required them to take an oath of allegiance to Augustus, and a good Jew could not bind himself by an oath. The Essenes absolutely refused all oaths, and Jesus expected the same of his disciples (Matt. 5:33–37). At the time of the census, six thousand Pharisees refused to swear the oath to Augustus, which sparked a wave of civil disobedience.

Several years later another event occurred, probably while Jesus' parents were still in Egypt. Herod had placed a golden eagle above the portal of the temple, which was a scandal for the Jews since all images, busts, and representations of any living thing were forbidden. Following the advice of two very prominent lawyers, some young men were lowered with ropes from the roof of the temple. In broad daylight, with crowds looking on, they demolished the golden eagle with axes. Forty instigators were arrested and brought before the king, who had them executed.[4]

Herod died shortly thereafter. Before dying, however, realizing that the Jews would rejoice at his death, he ordered that a sizable number of Judeans be arrested and put to death as soon as he died, "so that all the families of Judea will weep over me, whether they want to or not!"[5]

As soon as he inherited his father's throne, Archelaus was faced with a serious problem. The inhabitants of Jerusalem were demanding punishment for the high priest and officials who had failed to challenge Herod's orders and had permitted the executions of the lawyers and youth for destroying the eagle. As

Archelaus hesitated, an angry crowd gathered. In panic the king sent out his entire army and cavalry against them. Three thousand Jews were massacred. The others fled to the mountains.[6]

Some time later Antipas and Archelaus sailed for Rome to seek the emperor's arbitration in the matter of Herod's succession. While Archelaus was in Rome, Varus, legate of Syria, returned to Antioch after putting down the uprising. He left behind one legion (about six thousand men). He also left Sabinus (the procurator of Caesar Augustus' possessions) and ordered him to take an inventory of Herod's wealth.

Sabinus turned out to be unskilled and dishonest and relentlessly undertook the search for the king's treasures. Prompted by insatiable greed, he took the Jewish citadels by force. The pilgrims en route to Jerusalem for Pentecost organized themselves into three columns and besieged Sabinus and his legion in the royal palace. The porticoes of the temple became the scene of a desperate battle during which the Jews tried to crush the Romans with stones. But the Romans seized the treasures of the temple after setting the porticoes on fire and massacring many Jews. In so doing, Sabinus appropriated four hundred talents for himself.

Although the Jewish troops of Archelaus initially cooperated with the Romans to maintain order, when they saw the violation of the temple they were scandalized and sided with the insurrectionists. In no time, the land had been put to fire and to the sword. Sabinus alerted Varus, who returned to Palestine with two more legions and their four "wings" of cavalry. He came to the aid of the besieged legion in Jerusalem. In all, the Romans had twenty thousand well-trained men. The ten thousand Jews gathered in the mountains did not stand a chance of victory over such an army.

Then Achiab, Herod's cousin, intervened and succeeded in convincing the ten thousand Jews that their venture was senseless and stood no chance of success. The Jews were wise enough to follow his advice and capitulate. Varus proved himself generous. He set most of them free, except those members of the royal house who had taken part in the insurrection. As for the people who still tried to resist, Varus treated them with utmost cruelty: two thousand of them were crucified. He also ordered the destruction of Emmaus, a small town where Roman soldiers had been massacred.

It is quite possible that this event was recounted to Jesus as a child and convinced him of the futility of armed insurrection against Rome. Later, in a parable, he expressed it thus, "Suppose a king is about to go to war against another king. Will he not first sit down and consider whether he is able with ten thousand men to oppose the one coming against him with twenty thousand? If he is not able, he will send a delegation while the other is still a long way off and will ask for terms of peace" (Luke 14:31–32).

It was also during Jesus' youth that the most violent nationalistic party of all, the Zealots, was organized.[7] Its founder, Judas the Galilean (or Gaulanite), along with the Pharisee Zadok, preached disobedience and tax evasion.

Judas asserted himself as a capable leader. His first deed was the ransacking of the arsenal at Sepphoris in Galilee, a royal city a few kilometers north of Nazareth. Armed with the weapons he and his men seized there, he proclaimed himself king. Commenting on the movement, Josephus writes, "This school agrees in all other respects with the opinions of the Pharisees except that they have a passion for liberty that is almost unconquerable, since they are convinced that God alone is their leader and master. They think little of submitting to death in unusual forms…if only they may avoid calling any man master." This is why they refused to pay tribute to Caesar.[8]

No one knows what happened to Judas in the end. But neither Antipas nor the Romans ever completely succeeded in eliminating the Zealots. Twenty years after Judas, there were still a few around.

After Judas's death there were other pretenders to the throne. In Perea, Simon, one of Herod's ex-slaves, was proclaimed king and burned the palace in Jericho. After him, Athronges took the title of king and gathered a large crowd around him. He and his four brothers fought vigorously with the aim of slaughtering the Romans.[9] The Book of Acts, which also mentions Judas the Galilean, refers to a certain Theudas, who also tried to stir up the people.[10] It is noteworthy that when the famous Gamaliel, the apostle Paul's teacher, referred to Theudas and Judas the Galilean before the Sanhedrin, he compared them with Peter and John, who were also accused of sedition. In the eyes of the Sanhedrin, the first Christians were undoubtedly comparable to the patriots who attempted to deliver Israel.[11]

Several years after Jesus' death, the Zealots changed their tactics, went underground, and reappeared under the name of "Sicarii." Concealing daggers under their clothes, they mixed with the crowds during religious feasts and struck down Jewish nobility and elite whom they suspected of collaboration. Josephus writes, "The first to be assassinated by them was Jonathan, the high priest. After his death there were numerous murders daily. The panic created was more alarming than the calamity itself— everyone constantly expecting death, as on a battlefield. Men kept an eye on their enemies and would not even trust their friends when they approached. Yet even while their suspicions were aroused and they were on their guard, they still fell, so swift were the conspirators and so crafty in eluding detection."[12]

The Zealots and the Sicarii were not the only movements of this kind. Josephus notes the following:

> Besides these there arose another body of villains with purer hands but with more impious intentions...Deceivers and impostors under the pretence of divine inspiration fostering revolutionary changes, they led [the multitude] out into the desert under the belief that God would there give them tokens of deliverance.

A still worse blow was dealt to the Jews by the Egyptian false prophet. A charlatan who had gained for himself the reputation of a prophet, this man appeared in the country, collected a following of about thirty thousand dupes, and led them by a circuitous route from the desert to the Mount of Olives. From there he planned to force an entrance into Jerusalem and after overpowering the Roman garrison, to set himself up as ruler of the people... His attack was anticipated by Felix...The Egyptian escaped with a few of his followers; most of his force were killed or taken prisoners, the remainder dispersed.[13]

The Book of Acts mentions this Egyptian. After having arrested Paul during a riot in the temple, a Roman commander asked Paul, "Aren't you the Egyptian who started a revolt and led the four thousand terrorists out into the desert some time ago?" (Acts 21:38).

Social unrest, religious tensions, the stranglehold of injustice, a burning desire for ritual purity, and a passionate messianic hope were little by little carrying the people toward the final revolt. It broke out in A.D. 66, after the procurator Gessius Florus had crucified many Jews to repress the growing restlessness. Yet in the middle of all this tumult, another current was emerging, one to which Jesus would point his followers.

CHAPTER NINE

Seeds of Nonviolence

The intent of this book is not to describe the gradual fall of Jewish messianism into the violence that caused the destruction of Jerusalem. Its aim is rather to show that another current was emerging in troubled Palestine, one that would prove fertile ground for Jesus' message.

Revolutionary outbursts and subversive tactics aside, the behavior of most Jews in Israel during the Herodian-Roman period was by and large nonpolitical. They were consumed with eking out an existence. However, in addition to the various insurrectionary movements there were occasional acts of resistance of the nonviolent kind—usually directed against massive insults to the religious feelings of the larger Jewish populace. The attitude of most of Jesus' Jewish contemporaries was not that of the freedom fighters. It is difficult to know whether Jesus was influenced by them or whether he inspired them, but we know that for fifteen years, from the beginning of Pilate's rule until the end of the proconsulary regime in Judea (A.D. 26 to 41), the Jews in Palestine gave up combating violence with violence.

Nonviolent Resistance

Immediately after his arrival in Judea, a few months before Jesus began his ministry, Pilate made the mistake of bringing several military ensigns bearing the emperor's effigy into Jerusalem. This was a serious offense to the religious customs of the Jews, who forbade any representation of the human form. So the Jews rallied together, went to Caesarea, and begged Pilate to remove the ensigns. When Pilate refused, they initiated what today we would call a nonviolent demonstration; they lay down on the ground and stayed there for five days and nights.

The next day, Pilate took his seat on his tribunal in the large stadium and called the people together as if he were intending to answer them. At a given signal, his armed troops surrounded the Jews. When the Jews saw these troops massed around them in three rows, they remained silent. Then Pilate declared that they would be slaughtered if they refused to accept Caesar's images and motioned for the soldiers to draw their swords. But the protestors threw themselves to the ground together in tight rows, exposed their necks, and claimed they were ready to die rather than violate their faith. Astonished at the sight of such fervent religious zeal, Pilate ordered the ensigns to be immediately removed. Jewish nonviolent resistance had paid off![1]

Several years later Pilate was building an aqueduct to Jerusalem and seized the treasure of the temple to finance its construction. This violation aroused much protest. To disperse the demonstration, Pilate scattered "plainclothes soldiers" in the crowd. At a given signal, they began to beat the crowd unmercifully, but the crowd offered no resistance. The people let themselves be massacred without panic or weakness.[2]

A similar event took place three years after Pilate's dismissal. Here is the story. Caligula, Tiberius's successor, reigned only four years, but he was insane. He was the first Roman emperor to demand worship as a god. He awarded himself triumphs for imaginary victories and gave the title of consul to his horse. In A.D. 39, Caligula decided to send Petronius, the legate of Syria, to Jerusalem with three legions to install one of his statues in the temple. To the Jews, such a sacrilegious deed would have been an "abomination of the desolation," comparable to the time Antiochus Epiphanes installed a statue of Zeus in the temple—a recurrence Jesus had predicted.

A massive uprising was the only appropriate response to such a sacrilege. However, instead of taking up arms the Jews declared themselves ready to die in order to prevent this scandal. They organized something of a nationwide strike, stopped sowing their fields, and remained in front of the legate's house in Ptolemais for fifty days of passive resistance. Encouraged by their example, King Agrippa, a childhood friend of Caligula's, joined the intercessors. Upset and astounded by such unanimity, Petronius agreed, at the risk of his life, to intercede before the emperor. But Caligula was infuriated by his legate's disobedience and sent back a letter ordering him to commit suicide.

At this point providence showed its hand. Because of strong west winds the fatal letter reached Petronius twenty-seven days after he had received news of Caligula's murder by another source. Thus Petronius's life was saved. In this case, nonviolent resistance won over both the king and the Roman governor to the Jews' cause. The Jews gained an unexpected victory without bloodshed.[3]

This is not to say that such forms of resistance always worked. The time Pilate robbed the temple treasury to build an aqueduct, he brutally crushed the resistance. However, it is still striking to see how courageous nonviolent resistance can influence the adversary and how providential events, in this case Caligula's death, can appear as God's response to such acts of courage and faith.

It is likely that the splendid movement which nonviolently resisted Caligula's blasphemous orders nine years after Jesus' death was inspired by the first Christians, who at that time already filled Jerusalem and had even infiltrated the ranks of the Sanhedrin.

The Options

Among the various currents of thought and socio-political activity at the time of Jesus, three tendencies can be distinguished: collaboration, withdrawal, and resistance.[4]

Among the collaborators, the most prominent were the Herodians and the publicans, that is, those who served the occupation power and whose customs they had more or less adopted. This group was not very large and they were the employees and supporters of Herod Antipas's government. They hellenized their language, clothes, entertainment, games, and customs; everything was done according to Greco-Roman fashion. In the Gospels we see the Herodians making an alliance with the Pharisees to denounce and execute Jesus, although they were traditionally enemies of each other.

Also among the collaborators were the Sadducees and the chief priests, who made up the majority of the Sanhedrin in Jerusalem. They were conservatives, the guardians of worship in the temple – suspicious of anything that changed the religious customs – and did not participate in the political and religious awakening of the people. They did not believe in the coming of the Messiah nor were they expecting the reestablishment of the kingdom of Israel. They favored, by and large, a way of life that encouraged peaceful coexistence with the occupation forces. Both Annas and Caiaphas were Sadducees.

The Sadducees did not share the Pharisees' aversion to everything foreign. In general they had the confidence of the wealthy and were the principal beneficiaries of the system. They favored a compromise with Rome and were alarmed by the unrest caused by anything revolutionary—including Jesus' speeches—and they worked hard to keep their position of power and influence. Often the chief priest made impassioned appeals to the people not to challenge Roman rule. Although the vast majority of Jews in Israel were not aligned with any special group, the Sadducean attitude prevailed in Jerusalem and in all of Judea.

Among those who opted for withdrawal were the Pharisees and the Essenes. Meaning "separated ones," the Pharisees arose from the ranks of the people as a renewal movement. Their base was among the villages and the town synagogues. Their chief concern was ritual purity, which they believed was binding on all Jews, not just the priests. The Pharisees expectantly awaited Israel's deliverance, and some of them were even extremists with Zealot tendencies, who favored armed revolt. But the majority of them concentrated their energies on scrupulous adherence to the Mosaic Law, teaching strict observance of the Sabbath, fasts, purifications, prayers, tithes, and dietary ordinances. For guidance in applying the Law to everyday life, they turned to the scribes, scholars, and teachers who were formally trained in the study of the Law.

The Pharisees' concern and activity were religious and moral rather than political. By and large, they avoided direct political involvement, adopting an attitude of indifference regarding rulers and the way they ruled. They rarely aligned themselves with any of the factions, nor actively opposed Roman rule. However, as soon as an emperor or proconsul threatened to contaminate the temple, they brought their influence to bear against him and joined others in movements of resistance.[5]

Although "Pharisees" has taken on a pejorative connotation, their original intent was to fight the dissolving influence of Hellenism among Jews under the Hasmonaeans. But in their attempt to preserve the purity of the chosen people, they unfortunately imprisoned the Jewish people in a series of negative prescriptions that suffocated living faith and charity. But above all, their self-righteous spirit was destructive. They practiced such a strict moral censorship that it drove not only prostitutes, drunkards, and gluttons away from God, but also non-Jews, whom they shunned to keep from defiling their own ritual purity. This also included Jews who collaborated with the Gentiles to earn their livelihood, such as the publicans, toll-gatherers, and Herodians. The narrowness of the Pharisees' understanding of holiness, their way of confusing faith in God with external observances, and their neglect of the true riches of the heart caused Jesus to dissociate himself from them.[6]

Whereas the Pharisees' position was one of indifference, the Essenes opted for outright withdrawal. Except for a few enclaves in cities, they left society to live in the Judean desert. Like the Pharisees, they believed in the resurrection of the dead and individual salvation, but they formed a closed voluntary community of poverty of which one became a member by abandoning one's possessions. As "Sons of Light" they put all their hope in an apocalyptic battle that would someday bring God's victory over the "Sons of Darkness."

The Essenes remained celibate, were charitable toward the poor, and adopted the children of others. They did not take oaths except for the one they swore at the end of their probationary period. They did primarily agricultural work and rejected all professions that would have meant compromising with the world. Their monastic discipline included silence and obedience to the superiors they elected. Both before and after meals they frequently practiced ablutions that had a sacred character. They taught and practiced universal priesthood and established a network of friends from city to city. A traveling Essene was received as a guest by his brothers wherever he went. The Essenes practiced nonviolence up to a certain point. They submitted to the authorities, which they considered to be instituted by God. When they traveled, however, they carried weapons as protection against robbers.

There was much tension between the Essenes and the temple clergy. Asserting that the temple had been defiled by an unworthy priesthood, the Essenes offered no ritual sacrifices at the temple and considered justice and temperance to be the only true sacrifices God requests. In this respect, their teachings come close to those of the Old Testament prophets and of Jesus himself.[7]

The document called *The War of the Sons of Light and the Sons of Darkness* tells in symbolic form of the Essenes' messianic expectations and of the supreme battle between God and Satan that will bring about the final victory of the Sons of Light, God's allies. These warlike descriptions seem to imply that some young Essenes, tired of the nonviolence practiced by their order, may have joined the ranks of the Zealots that engaged in armed rebellion. They thought the hour of the final struggle between Yahweh and the Gentiles had come. The Essenes' participation in the revolt of A.D. 66 would explain the destruction of their convent at Qumran by the Romans and the disappearance of their order after A.D. 70.

John the Baptist's austerity, his preaching in the desert (where he lived as the Essenes did), and the baptism of purification he practiced seem to indicate Essene influence. And some of Jesus' instructions to his disciples recall Essene ordinances.[8] Their influence on him (perhaps through John the Baptist) cannot be denied. However, there are many profound differences. Jesus did not encourage his disciples to lead a monastic life. Instead, he made them messengers, preachers, and apostles. And as we shall see, Jesus was more radically nonviolent than the Essenes, even forbidding his disciples to carry a stick in order to defend themselves from robbers during their travels (Matt. 10:10). Finally, the idea of a final battle between the Sons of Light and the Sons of

Darkness—a very tempting idea for the Jews of Jesus' time who expected a Messiah—can be found neither in Jesus' teachings nor in the teachings of the apostles.

In addition to collaboration and withdrawal, there were groups who chose the path of outright resistance, which can be divided into three categories. In the first category, resistance amounted to cultural opposition in general, particularly to hellenization. This meant refusal to offer pagan sacrifices, to hold administrative positions in local government, and to do military service. This kind of resistance created ghettos in various Mediterranean cities.

In Israel itself, resistance sprang from a piety and devotion that awaited Israel's deliverance. The Messiah was at the door. Rumors circulated: he is here; he is there; he is Judas the Galilean; he is John the Baptist, Jesus of Nazareth, Theudas the Egyptian prophet. Some patriots proclaimed themselves king, retreated to the mountains and hid in caves, coming out only to ambush the Romans or assassinate Jews who collaborated with the occupation forces. Some Pharisees followed their example and joined the final revolt in A.D. 66.

But there was yet a third type of resistance, stemming from the tradition of the great prophets who expected the coming of the "Servant of the Lord," the "Prince of Peace," meek and humble of heart, the founder of the kingdom of God on earth. To this group belong John the Baptist's parents, the priest Zechariah and his wife, Elizabeth; Mary, Jesus' mother, and Joseph, her husband; the prophetess Anna and the aged Simeon; and "all who were looking forward to the redemption of Jerusalem," as Luke describes their hope (Luke 1–2).

Could the religious faith, civic courage, and political realism that the prophets had exemplified be revived? What new prophet would be capable of leading his people toward a far-reaching reform of habits and consciences? Who would rid Judaism of its formalism and its rabbinical literalism and bring it back to its primitive purity? Who would lead a total revolution that would shake off internal oppression as well as the foreign yoke? These are the questions Jesus answered by proclaiming himself messianic king and liberator.

Jesus' approach stood in unique opposition to the prevailing assumptions of his day.[9] He articulated an altogether different way, as we will see.[10] He did not come in the sectarian guise of his time, offering redemption only to those belonging to a particular group (e.g., Pharisees, Essenes, Zealots, and the like), nor did he adopt a primarily adversarial stance. He came with a prophetic message concerned for the good of all and with an eagerness to bring God's kingdom within reach of everybody, even the enemy.

CHAPTER TEN

Another Way

As we have seen, Jesus came proclaiming the kingdom of God, inaugurated by a Jubilee. This Jubilee upset both human tradition and religious scruples. Consequently, Jesus' adversaries tried to kill him. They were determined to prevent a dangerous revolution that would usurp their influence and power. Jesus seemingly had only two alternatives: violent resistance or flight into the desert–the Zealot temptation of force or the Essene option of withdrawal. But Jesus chose to do neither. He overcame the temptations of revolt and escape, but did so at the cost of a great struggle.[1]

The Zealot Temptation

The Zealots were preparing themselves to wage a war of liberation against Rome. They were extremists who occasionally used their daggers against the occupation forces and sometimes against countrymen whom they suspected of collaboration. After having assassinated those who favored collaboration with Rome one by one, they finally succeeded in sweeping the entire nation into a generalized war in A.D. 66.[2]

Jesus was not exempt from being tempted by the solution of force. It appears, for example, that there were Zealots among Jesus' disciples: Simon, called the Zealot, and probably Judas Iscariot.[3] We also know that from a high mountain he saw "all the kingdoms of the world," and that the tempter said, "If you worship me, it will all be yours" (Luke 4:5). Jesus knew the miraculous power at his disposal. He also knew that with this power he could dominate the world if he used the means every conqueror used: military might, money, prestige, and fear. But he rejected this possibility.

Jesus also knew that with God's bread he could feed the hungry of the world. This temptation seemed to haunt Jesus at several points in his ministry. One day in Galilee, as the Passover was approaching, Jesus took pity on the hungry crowd and miraculously fed them (John 6:1–15). The Zealots became quite enthusiastic. They were convinced they had at last found the Messiah and wanted to take him away to make him king. But Jesus overcame the temptation to power. He escaped and withdrew to the mountain to be alone.

This same temptation to power harassed him when Simon Peter enthusiastically exclaimed, "You are the Christ, the Son of the living God." Jesus answered Peter by explaining that he would be put to death, and that he would not resist his enemies because his death was part of God's plan (Matt. 16:16–21). But Peter said, "Never, Lord! This shall never happen to you!" One can well imagine Peter meaning: "We, your disciples, will not allow this to happen; we will fight for you!" or "Do not let yourself be murdered! Let us retreat into the Judean mountains, among the Zealots or the Essenes, where the police cannot reach us." Jesus' impatient reaction reveals the dramatic nature of his own inner struggle. He answered the tempter as he had previously on the mountaintop, "Get behind me, Satan! You are a stumbling block to me; you do not have in mind the things of God, but the things of men."

Despite this moral victory, Jesus was still faced with the temptation of using violence. It can be felt in the curses he spoke against
Capernaum, Korazin, and Bethsaida after they rejected him.
To the extent that Jesus was announcing the kingdom of God
on earth and proclaiming the Jubilee, he met the obstacle all revolutionaries encounter: the spiteful and violent reaction of the
conservatives, the guardians of the old institutions and privileges.[4]
Jesus saw that the success of his undertaking was in jeopardy. To
keep it from failing, would he have to abbreviate the long and difficult pilgrimage of justice in history and impose the kingdom of
God on the rebellious by force? Such a decision would have been
made, of course, for the good of all, even of Jesus' enemies. After
the establishment of the kingdom, they would have been the first
to join him and congratulate him for his initiative.

One gets the distinct feeling that Jesus was on the verge of
Jesus understood that what was at stake would demand a deci-
sive struggle. It is therefore not surprising to find the word "hate"
in Jesus' vocabulary when he refers to certain necessary separa-
tions. "If anyone comes to me," he once said, "and does not hate
his father and mother, his wife and children, his brothers and
sisters—yes, even his own life—he cannot be my disciple" (Luke
14:26).

One gets the distinct feeling that Jesus was on the verge of
making a warlike decision when he exclaimed that he would cast
fire upon the earth and swing the sword that brings division: "Do
you think I came to bring peace on earth? No, I tell you, but
division. From now on there will be five in one family divided
against each other, three against two and two against three. They
will be divided, father against son and son against father, mother
against daughter and daughter against mother, mother-in-law
against daughter-in-law and daughter-in-law against mother-in-
law" (Luke 12:49–53). Jesus understood well that God's rulership

would first require upheaval. In some way or another it would have to be taken by force.

At one point Jesus said, "From the days of John the Baptist until now, the kingdom of heaven has been forcefully advancing, and forceful men lay hold of it" (Matt. 11:12). However one chooses to interpret these words, they still reveal Jesus' sympathy for "forceful" people. According to some interpreters, this passage means that Jesus thought only those with a violent character could force the door to the kingdom of God and become its heroes. Jesus' disciples were to be combatants who would fight for Israel's independence like the Zealots. According to others, Jesus' words are actually a warning against those who want to establish the kingdom of God by violence. Regardless, they reveal a profound irritation with the "lukewarm," who think that one can enter the kingdom of God without struggle.

Toward the end of his life, the temptation toward violence only increased. Jesus vented his indignation toward the scribes and Pharisees by calling divine vengeance upon them (Matthew 23). The parables he employed almost all conclude with violence. Some tenants revolt against the heir of the vineyard, and Jesus said, "He [the master] will bring those wretches to a wretched end" (Matt. 21:41). Of those who had been invited to attend the wedding feast of the king's son but refused, Jesus remarked, "The king was enraged and he sent his army and destroyed those murderers and burned their city." This same king tells his servants, "Tie him [the man who had no wedding garment] hand and foot and throw him outside into the darkness, where there will be weeping and gnashing of teeth" (Matt. 22:7, 13).

One could argue that these are only parables, imagery used to make an impression on the listeners and bring them to repentance. But to destroy corrupt customs that turned the temple into a marketplace, Jesus took a whip of cords and chased out those who sold and bought in the temple. He overturned the tables of the money-changers and the seats of those who sold pigeons and said, "My house will be called a house of prayer, but you are making it a den of robbers" (Matt. 21:13).

The temptation to use violence accompanied Jesus right to his death. A few hours before his arrest he went so far as to reverse his earlier instructions concerning absolute poverty and meekness. "But now if you have a purse, take it, and also a bag; and if you don't have a sword, sell your cloak and buy one." When his disciples said, "See, Lord, here are two swords," he told them, "That is enough" (Luke 22:36–38). Beyond these two paltry human weapons, Jesus knew he could count on the help of twelve legions of angels ready to intervene at a moment's notice. It was only after an intense inner struggle, after the genuine moral agony at Gethsemane, that Jesus finally rejected resorting to violence.[5]

Jesus was no theorist of nonviolence. He overcame violence by a succession of day-to-day decisions and a series of redemptive acts. On every occasion, he freely chose the road of nonviolence rather than that of armed resistance. Jesus' refusal to use force was therefore not some extra-historical dream of a mystic trying to forget the concrete realities of this world. He did not ignore the human condition. His way was a step-by-step journey through the obstacles, mountain passes, snares, and cliffs of history. Jesus carved a new path into the hardness of human realities, a path he trod first, carrying on his shoulders the way of the cross and all the requirements of the kingdom of God: social justice, radical transformation, commitment to truth, and personal regeneration. These are the materials with which he builds the kingdom of God.

Consequently, the chastisement deserved by the hypocritical Pharisees, the jealous Sanhedrin, the cowardly Pilate, and the fickle crowd fell back on him. Jesus deliberately chose to be crucified. He took responsibility for the apparent failure of his mission.

But his sacrifice was not a capitulation. For since that event, no man, no nation, no party, no head of state, whether a believer or an unbeliever, can forget Christ. No one can honestly ignore the fact that it was God himself who was nailed to the cross with our injustices and crimes.

The Way of Withdrawal\

If Jesus was faced with the temptation to use violence, it is also true that at certain points he was tempted to give up all public activity, retire to the desert, and form a community of the faithful, separate from the world.

Several factors pushed Jesus toward this. First, he was baptized by John the Baptist, who was a prophet from the desert, under the strong influence of the Essene monks. Like the Essenes, John the Baptist reechoed Isaiah's call: "A voice calling in the desert, 'Prepare the way for the Lord; make straight paths for him'" (Matt. 3:3– Isa. 40:3). Like the Essenes, John also expected the coming of the Messiah. However, John the Baptist indiscriminately baptized all those who came to him with a repentant mind, whereas the Essenes formed a closed congregation and considered themselves alone to be the "penitents of the desert."

Jesus was sympathetic with the ministry of John the Baptist. Like him, he lived for a while in the desert. Like him, he preached a message of repentance. And like John, Jesus recruited his disciples from among men whom the Essenes considered impure. Neither did he advise them to practice ablutions, fasts, or separation from women, or to retreat to the desert.

Nevertheless, the Gospels do reveal a certain anguish on the part of Jesus. On the one hand, Jesus dedicated himself completely to the crowds in order to accomplish the salvation of the destitute. On the other, he seems to have been overcome by a nostalgia for solitude from time to time, and also by the desire to form a small faithful community away from the world, to wait for the glorious return of the Son of Man.

Once, for example, Jesus was going down the mountain the day after his transfiguration. As he entered the crowd, he heard the complaint of a man whose son was epileptic, "I brought him to your disciples but they could not heal him." Jesus grew impatient with the powerlessness of his disciples and the unending requests of the crowd and exclaimed, "O unbelieving and perverse generation, how long shall I stay with you? How long shall I put up with you?" (Matt. 17:17). And with this same aversion for the crowd, Jesus enjoined his disciples not to give holy things to dogs, and not to throw pearls before swine (Matt. 7:6).

On another occasion, Jesus used some very strange words, whose importance we tend to forget, to explain to his disciples why he spoke in parables. Parables were generally used to express some profound spiritual truth in a more accessible form. But, strangely enough, the crowd failed to understand one of Jesus' simpler parables, the parable of the sower. Jesus concludes by telling his listeners, "He who has ears, let him hear" (Matt. 13:9). After the crowd had dispersed, his close friends and the twelve disciples questioned him, "Why do you speak to the people in parables?" And Jesus answered with these mysterious words, "The secret of the kingdom of God has been given to you. But to those on the outside everything is said in parable so that, 'they may be ever seeing but never perceiving, and ever hearing but never understanding; otherwise they might turn and be forgiven!'" (Mark 4:10–12). Here again one feels Jesus' impatience with "those outside."

The Gospel of Mark goes on to say, "With many similar parables Jesus spoke the word to them, as much as they could understand. He did not say anything to them without using a parable. But when he was alone with his own disciples, he explained everything"

(Mark 4:33–34). Such texts place Jesus much closer to the Essenes than one might first think. He, too, was gathering around him a small group of disciples, an inner circle to whom he gave secrets the crowd was not able to receive.

Jesus' words echo the prophet Isaiah. God instructed Isaiah to "Make the heart of this people calloused; make their ears dull and close their eyes…" For how long? "Until the cities lie ruined and without inhabitant…But as the terebinth and oak leave stumps when they are cut down, so the holy seed will be the stump in the land" (Isa. 6:10–13).

Having experienced the incomprehensible indifference of the people, Jesus prophesied, like Isaiah, that the majority of his listeners would not be converted, but would be hardened by his message. However, their hardness of heart would not hold God back, because God uses failures and transforms them into victories. Like the holy seed that was to come from the Jewish people after the destruction of Jerusalem, the disciples to whom Jesus disclosed the secret of the kingdom of God would be the first fruits, the birth of a new people.

Jesus seems to vacillate between a widespread call to the crowd on the one hand, and a way reserved only for a small group of elect on the other. "There is nothing concealed that will not be disclosed, or hidden that will not be made known. What I tell you in the dark, speak in the daylight; what is whispered in your ear, proclaim from the roofs" (Matt. 10:26–27). "But small is the gate and narrow the road that leads to life, and only a few find it" (Matt. 7:14).

Why did Jesus forbid the demons he expelled and the people he healed to announce that he was the Messiah (Mark 1:34; 3:12; etc.)? He did not want to be mistaken for a military messiah, such as the Jews were expecting. The indiscretion of a leper he had healed, for instance, hindered his activities (Mark 1:44–45). He could no longer openly enter a town and had to confine himself to the country. He preferred to withdraw to the desert in order to avoid this confusion.

In fact, it appears that Jesus liked to escape to the desert to pray. Sometimes he went there alone, sometimes with his disciples. Indiscrete crowds of people often followed them there (Mark 3:7–12). Jesus would then give in to their persistence and teach them while healing the sick.

But the desert became both a refuge and a temptation to Jesus, especially at the end of his ministry, when he moved the focus of his work from Galilee to Judea. He had lived in a village called Aenon, not far from the place where John the Baptist had baptized him. It was there that Jesus' disciples baptized for the first time, after the manner of John the Baptist (John 3:22–23).

Toward the end of his ministry, Jesus came back to this same area, in the footsteps of his forerunner whom Herod had decapitated, as if he were attempting to return to the beginning of his work. A few days earlier in Jerusalem he had openly proclaimed that he was the Christ. The Jewish authorities had tried to seize him in order to stone him, but he had escaped and come to Aenon. It is quite likely Jesus was tempted to remain there permanently, far from the struggles of history, because "in that place many believed in Jesus" (John 10:41–42). Was it not better to give up trying to convert the masses who rejected him, in order to gather the "remnant" of the faithful in the desert?

After having interrupted his retreat to perform the miracle that upset Jerusalem, the raising to life of Lazarus at Bethany, Jesus once again disappeared. The Sanhedrin threatened him with death. And so he no longer went about openly among the Jews, but went from there to a region near the wilderness to stay with his disciples (John 11:54).

In the end, Jesus would not go the way of withdrawal. As the last act of the drama drew near, a more pressing matter than the founding of a small sect summoned him. Jesus would go to Jerusalem, for the sake of Israel. He would go to the temple and assert his prerogatives as messianic King. He would come to gather God's children together as a hen gathers her chicks under her wings (Luke 13:34).

Jesus' Entry into History

Jesus stood between – and, in the end, beyond – the options of violence or withdrawal, fight or flight. As tempting as these options were, he chose another way. This does not mean he refused to play a historical role. We must not imagine him as a sublime yogi sheltered from the world on the shores of eternity, or as an ascetic who invited his disciples to follow him in solitude in order to learn an ideal having no connection whatsoever with the problems of this world.[6] To extol the exceptional nature of his holiness to such a degree is but an evasion of discipleship.

True, Jesus told Pilate that his kingship was "not of this world," for if it were, his servants would fight (John 18:36). People generously concede to the advocates of peace that Jesus was therefore nonviolent, since he did not permit his followers to shed blood for his protection. This is self-evident. But to then immediately go on to argue that the kingdom of God, of which Jesus is the champion, is a purely spiritual kingdom, completely unrelated to the realities of this world, misinterprets the threat Jesus posed to Pilate and his contemporaries entirely. Jesus' message is skewed whenever it is argued that as a Christian one should not bear arms, but that as a citizen of the state one is nevertheless obligated to participate in the armed defense of the common good.[7]

Such an interpretation of Jesus' teaching demonstrates a severe lack of understanding as to why Jesus came in the first place. Indeed, in John's Gospel, to be in the world but "not of the world" has little to do with belonging to an invisible, otherworldly kingdom. To be "not of the world" simply means not conforming to the spirit of the age in which we live. Such nonconformity will invariably provoke hatred. Hence Jesus' words, "If you belonged to the world, it would love you as its own. As it is, you do not belong to the world, but I have chosen you out of the world. That is why the world hates you" (John 15:19).

Jesus' mission was certainly for this earth. "My prayer is not that you take them out of the world but that you protect them from the evil one" (John 17:15). The Messiah had both feet on the ground, right where he wanted his kingdom to be, especially among his disciples.

In fact, in Greek the passage "My kingdom is not of this world" means literally "My kingdom is not of this source." In other words, Jesus' kingdom does not have the same origin as those of this world, nor can it be won by the same means.[8] This is why Jesus expects his followers to transcend what is humanly possible. The final section of this book will explore more fully the relationship between Christ's kingdom, which is not of this fallen order, and the world in which we live, to which the Roman Empire, represented by Pilate, belonged.

What, then, is the task of the Messiah's servants? In short, they will continue the work Jesus began. "As you sent me into the world, I have sent them into the world" (John 17:18). Certainly, this mandate will not be easy to carry out. It will spark opposition. But, says Jesus, the reign of the prince of this world (the power of darkness) is transitory. "The prince of this world now stands condemned...In this world you will have trouble. But take heart! I have overcome the world" (John 16:11, 33).

Jesus overcomes the world not by condemning it, but by saving it (John 3:16–18). He does not offer us an abstract kingdom of ideas, but redemptive actions of healing and liberation. Jesus came from God and returned to God, but only after having planted the seeds of the future: the kingdom on this earth. And Jesus the Messiah will return, because his final aim is to save the entire cosmos. There will be redemption, not just for individuals, but for the whole world. His kingdom will come fully to the earth, just as it is in heaven.

Jesus rejected the way of violence.[9] He overcame his enemies without using the methods common to the kingdoms of this world. His way would be the cross. And yet this way was not one of passive resignation or of avoiding conflict. To inaugurate his triumph as a peaceable king, he entered Jerusalem, the heart of humanity's anguish and longing. And he did so free from the temptations of coercion and withdrawal. Followed by the long procession of his disciples, Jesus made his entry into the history of each nation and of each century, and continues to do so through his people until the day when his victory will be complete.

CHAPTER ELEVEN

The Radical Explosion

We have seen how Jesus proclaimed a unique revolution. Unlike his contemporaries he refused to resist evil on its own terms. His kingdom was not of this world, yet it was for this world. This chapter will show how, although Jesus' thought developed from peculiarly Jewish premises, it expanded into a radically inclusive vision, which, in turn, would preclude violence.

Jesus remained faithful to Jewish forms of worship celebrated in the temple at Jerusalem. Although he emphasized that God delighted in mercy and not in sacrifices, he did not in principle exclude sacrifices. He did not abolish ritual, but rather enlarged its scope: "First go and be reconciled to your brother; then come and offer your gift" (Matt. 5:23–24).

His attitude toward circumcision was similar. He did not abolish it, but compared it with a physical healing, thus giving it a more human and less ritualistic meaning (John 7:22–24). Until the end Jesus, like every other orthodox Jew, regularly traveled to Jerusalem at the prescribed times to perform his religious duties in the temple. His criticism was not aimed at the temple, but rather at the priests and Levites, who were so consumed with their dogmatic preoccupations that they ignored those wounded by the side of the road. Contrary to the accusation made during his trial (Mark 14:58), Jesus did not desire the destruction of the temple, but its purification. The day of his messianic entry into Jerusalem, his burning zeal for the temple incited him to drive out the merchants: "My house will be called a house of prayer, but you are making it a den of robbers" (Matt. 21:13).

All this confirms that Jesus saw himself as the Jewish Messiah. He intended to reform the Jewish faith and understood his three-fold (religious, social, political) revolution within the context of the Jewish people. Jesus was a man of his time. However, his vision extended far beyond Jewish confines. Without ever softening his message or abandoning the Jewish concept of election, he allowed this notion of election to "explode" under the shock of new situations. His revolution transgressed boundaries his contemporaries refused to cross—boundaries that relegated certain people to the outside. God's work could not be boxed in; salvation must be extended to all.

To the Gentiles

The Jews of Jesus' day believed that they were destined to be a special blessing to all peoples. Non-Jewish nations would one day learn the way to Jerusalem, but only after Israel was purified. For this reason, Jesus commanded his disciples to go nowhere among the Gentiles. If we bear in mind that the Syrophoenician border was only eighteen miles away from Capernaum and that the Syrophoenicians still worshiped, under a veneer of Hellenism, such crude gods as Baal, Ashtoreth, and Melkart, the meaning of this command is unequivocal.

But Jesus did not blindly embrace his people's ethnic ideology. On several occasions he openly admired the faith of his Gentile listeners. In fact, three times out of eight recorded in the Gospels it was non-Jews who aroused his admiration. Take, for example, the well-known episode of the Syrophoenician woman. Jesus had taken refuge in pagan territory because the Herodians and the Pharisees were persecuting him. He was outside Jewish territory, in a place where idols were not banned and the environment was coarse and immoral. Those who have visited Baalbek (the ancient Heliopolis contemporary with dawning Christianity) – with its gigantic temples dedicated to the sun god Baal; to Bacchus, the god of drunkenness; and to Venus, the goddess of sensuality – will admit that maintaining the purity of Jewish worship and customs in this context was a permanent miracle. They can also imagine the horror Israelites might have felt at the thought of mixing with people who participated in such cultic practices.

Jesus must have experienced this feeling of horror when he was a refugee in the district of Tyre and Sidon. "He entered a house and did not want anyone to know it…" (Mark 7:24). It was here that a certain event especially upset him. A pagan woman, whose daughter was cruelly tortured by a demon, heard about Jesus and threw herself at his feet crying out, "Lord, Son of David, have mercy on me!" (Matt 15:21–28).

Jesus did not think it necessary to answer her plea. He said nothing. A Jew did not have any relations with Gentiles. Moreover, his disciples were annoyed by the woman's insistence and told Jesus to send her away. Then Jesus, to discourage her, said, "I was sent only to the lost sheep of Israel." These are the same terms he used when sending out his disciples (Matt. 10:5–6). But the woman insisted. Then Jesus answered with an expression that was probably a Jewish proverb, "It is not right to take the children's bread and toss it to their dogs."

What did this answer mean? It was surely not meant as an insult. It simply meant, "I, the Messiah of the Jews, am called to take care of my people. I was not sent to the Gentiles." By speaking in this way, Jesus was expressing the religious worldview of his fellow Jews. His starting point was the chosen people.

But the woman would not back down and answered Jesus with a bold remark. "Yes, Lord," she said, "but even the dogs eat the crumbs that fall from their masters' table." This reply was full of good sense and courage and it thoroughly impressed Jesus. Indeed, if there was enough for the children of Israel to eat, and more, how could he keep the Gentiles from taking part in the feast? For her reply, Jesus told the woman, "Woman, you have great faith! Your request is granted." And when she returned home, she found her daughter healed.

By breaking into the closed world of the Jewish people, the Syro-phoenician woman had unknowingly participated in the foundation of Christ's revolution, later to be termed Christianity. On that day, the kingdom of God ceased to be a promise reserved for Israel alone. One will not enter into it by birth only, but also by faith. The "violent ones," whose faith is able to remove mountains, will grasp it.

Samaritans Included

Jesus also shared current opinions about the Samaritans. The Samaritans were not of Jewish origin. They had come from Mesopotamia as colonists to replace the Jews at the time of the Babylonian exile and had adopted the worship of Yahweh. Upon their return from exile, the Jews forbade them to participate in the reconstruction of the temple, so they built a rival temple on Mount Gerizim. From that time on, Samaria was always an obstacle between Judea and Galilee for the Jews. Border incidents were common.

The Samaritans, for their part, also made relations with the Jews difficult at best. Once, for example, Samaritans secretly entered Jerusalem and dumped human bones under the temple's porticoes. After that incident, Samaritans were forbidden to enter the temple, which was now guarded with more vigilance.[1]

After Jesus' death the inhabitants of a small Samaritan town assassinated a Jew who was on the way to Jerusalem for the Passover. On hearing the news in Jerusalem, a Jewish mob spontaneously rushed to Samaria and massacred the inhabitants of the border towns, which they then set on fire. The leading figures of Jerusalem and the governor Cumanus had to intervene before peace could be reestablished. All who were arrested were crucified or decapitated.[2]

The Samaritan border was fifteen miles away from the Sea of Galilee. To get to Jerusalem one had to cross Samaria or take a lengthy detour, either along the Jordan or along the Mediterranean. Jesus traveled constantly by foot between Galilee and Jerusalem but, to our knowledge, he went through Samaria on only two occasions. In his first instructions to his disciples, he commanded, "Enter no town of the Samaritans, but go rather to the lost sheep of the house of Israel."

But Jesus' thinking toward the Samaritans did not confine itself to the current animosity. Once he crossed Samaria and sat down outside the town of Sychar, on the edge of a well, and sent his disciples into town for food. While at the well he met a person who had the double disadvantage of being both a woman and a Samaritan.

Jesus asked her for water. After a series of questions and answers about "living water," Jesus reminded the woman that "salvation is from the Jews" (John 4:22). But he also told her that genuine worship would please God regardless of where one worshipped. Troubled by these revelations and by Jesus' words about her loose life, the woman understood that she was talking to a prophet and declared that she, too, was waiting for the Messiah. When Jesus told her he was the one she was expecting, she left her water jar and ran into town to tell the people, who in turn came out to meet Jesus.

This simple conversation led to a pressing invitation. The inhabitants of Sychar pleaded with Jesus to stay with them. Jesus accepted the invitation and stayed with them for two days. The result was that many Samaritans from that town believed. One can only wonder whether Sychar was not the site of the first truly Christian church. Jesus' words spoken to the Samaritan seem to summarize the essence of the matter: "A time is coming and has now come when the true worshippers will worship the Father in spirit and truth, for they are the kind of worshippers the Father seeks. God is spirit, and his worshippers must worship in spirit and in truth" (John 4:23–24).

Long after this event, Jesus again went through Samaria. Far from refraining to enter the Samaritan cities, he now asked for hospitality and sent messengers ahead to prepare lodging for him. Ironically, this time it was the Samaritans who refused him lodging. By asking the Samaritans for hospitality, Jesus was extending the hand of friendship toward them. But they turned him away like an enemy! James and John took the blow very hard. The Samaritans' resistance exasperated them. They even asked Jesus' permission to order lightning to come down and destroy them. But Jesus outright refused to authorize the use of murderous violence. "You do not know what kind of spirit you are of, for the son of man did not come to destroy lives, but to save them" (Luke 9:55–56).[3]

Jesus' sympathy for the Samaritans meant one sure thing: God's liberation was exploding through barriers that had separated people. It is hardly surprising that Jewish nationalists suggested that Jesus was a Samaritan (John 8:48). Nationalists of all times have accused those who stand above their quarrels of belonging to the enemy.

One day, as Jesus was passing by the border between Samaria and Galilee, he healed ten lepers. But he was saddened by their lack of gratitude. The only one who returned to thank him was a Samaritan. Jesus exclaimed, "Were not all ten cleansed? Where are the other nine? Was no one found to return and give praise to God except this foreigner?" And so Jesus said to the Samaritan, "Rise and go; your faith has made you well" (Luke 17:17–19). Here was not only a physical healing, but also acceptance of a Samaritan into the kingdom of God.

The Romans

After opening the kingdom of God to the Samaritans, Jesus went on to invite the Romans to take part in God's kingdom. The story of Jesus' meeting with the centurion of Capernaum is too well known to be narrated at great length. This story is significant in light of the fact that Jesus, like all other devout Jews, most likely never set foot in the Roman city of Tiberias. When he went from the shores of the Sea of Galilee to the Jordan, he almost certainly bypassed this impure obstacle, which had been built on a cemetery.

According to Matthew 8:5–13, the centurion himself came to Jesus saying, "Lord, my servant lies at home paralyzed and in terrible suffering." According to Luke's version, however, the centurion approached Jesus by means of an intermediary (Luke 7:2–10). This is not surprising, since the Roman would have known that according to Jewish custom a rabbi such as Jesus could have no contact with pagans like him. So the centurion, who most probably had friends among the Jewish elders of Capernaum, sent them to the prophet as proxies. It seems that the elders themselves had some trouble convincing the Messiah. They pleaded with him urgently and tried to prove that this centurion was no ordinary Roman. "This man deserves to have you do this, because he loves our nation and has built our synagogue."

As Jesus was approaching his house, the centurion himself, who knew that a Hebrew rabbi would not touch a Gentile, repeated,

"Lord, don't trouble yourself, for I do not deserve to have you come under my roof. That is why I did not even consider myself worthy to come to you." This remark was not a display of personal inferiority, but rather of a shrewd knowledge of Judaism. Indeed, the centurion did not hesitate to compare himself with Jesus. He, as a soldier, obeyed his superiors without question and submitted to military discipline. His inferiors, in turn, owed him complete obedience and submission at every moment. Thus it seemed natural to the centurion that a Jewish prophet would heal his servant since he had authority over demons.

Jesus was surprised by the confidence the Roman had in him. From this he concluded, "I tell you the truth, I have not found anyone in Israel with such great faith. I say to you that many will come from the east and the west, and will take their places at the feast with Abraham, Isaac, and Jacob in the kingdom of heaven."

Here again we witness a radical religious revolution. At the very hour when the Jewish people were about to exclude themselves from the kingdom of God, non-Jews were entering into the kingdom, reserved until then only for the descendants of Abraham. Jesus concluded with sadness, "The subjects of the kingdom will be thrown outside, into the darkness, where there will be weeping and gnashing of teeth." But to the centurion, Jesus said, "Go! It will be done just as you believed it would." And the servant was healed at that very moment.

The Gospels never tell us if Jesus then went to the centurion's house. Nor do they mention the centurion's conversion. For all we know, the officer continued to practice his Roman religion and go about his military duties. Yet Jesus clearly acknowledged that sheep from other folds were entering the kingdom. The walls of established religion were crumbling under the weight of God's advancing kingdom.

Attitude toward Women

If we leave the domain of religious and racial prejudices, we can find that Jesus had to overcome yet another reservation. It was not a Jewish custom to keep company with persons of the opposite sex.[4] This is why his disciples were surprised when they found him in conversation with a woman at the well. Hadn't Jesus taught them not to look lustfully at a woman, lest they commit adultery (Matt. 5:28–29)? Had he not spoken of the voluntary celibacy he imposed on himself for the sake of the kingdom (Matt. 19:12)?

And yet Jesus showed that women were included in the kingdom of God. He welcomed the women who followed him in his travels, received him in their homes, and accompanied him to his execution. Some of these women even provided financial assistance. Jesus not only accepted this help, he did so without bothering about public opinion.[5]

Surprisingly enough, the more virtuous women, such as Jesus' mother and sisters or his disciples' wives, were not always the ones to enter the intimate circle of the disciples. Jesus painfully alluded to the necessity of breaking with one's family.[6]

On the other hand, there was a whole group of women who entered the narrow door to the kingdom who were scorned by everyone else: sick ones who touched his robe, abandoned widows, and even prostitutes. Yes, Jesus, the one who exhorted his followers to be careful how they looked at women, allowed himself to be touched by a prostitute (Luke 7:36–50). And touched in what a way! Tears to wet his feet, a head of hair to wipe them, kisses to revere them, an alabaster vase to pour out very expensive perfume. Simon, the Pharisee who had invited Jesus for a meal that day, was scandalized. His attitude may be justified. How many suspicions must have crossed his mind, the least of them being: "If this man were a prophet, he would know who is touching him and what kind of woman she is – that she is a sinner."

But in the somewhat alarming enthusiasm of the prostitute, Jesus discerned one of the principal virtues of the kingdom of God, a virtue he placed even above faith because it resembles God most—namely, love. We do not know the nature of the woman's love for Jesus. Did she recognize him as the Messiah, the Son of God who was capable of purifying her? Or was she simply overwhelmed upon meeting for the first time a genuinely pure man who treated her like a sister or a friend? Whatever the case may be, her tears were not only tears of admiration, but also tears of repentance mixed with a passionate desire for forgiveness.

In Jesus' revolution the traditional categories of "pure" and "impure" were totally upset, the notion of holiness utterly transformed. Simon, with his pure hands, was the impure one because he need-ed only a little forgiveness and felt only a little respect and a little thankfulness for the Savior. The prostitute, on the other hand, was the one who became truly pure. She was transformed by faith. Through Jesus, the woman had seen God and attached herself to him. And to her Jesus pronounced the great word of eternal life: "Your faith has saved you; go in peace."[7]

From one stage to another, Jesus' thought expanded until it exploded into a universal love for all people—especially the despised and rejected. His was not a universalism that mixed together all concepts, beliefs, and religions into the melting pot of tolerance. Jesus did not abolish the divine banquet where, according to Jewish tradition, Abraham, Isaac, and Jacob are seated. He simply invited to this banquet those relegated to the outside, those who responded to his invitation by showing love and faith in God.

Until the very end Jesus never renounced his privilege of being the Anointed One. Nevertheless, he destroyed the wall that separated non-Jews from the God of Israel. He became the new and living way by which all people have access to the kingdom of God.

And by acting in this way he removed every pretext for the use of violence. There would be no "us" versus "them." God's grace was offered to all, and with it the hand of fellowship and the offer of reconciliation.

CHAPTER TWELVE

The Sword of the Spirit

If boundaries between peoples needed erasing, then so, too, did practices and institutions that oppressed the human spirit. Sadly, those among Jesus' contemporaries who should have recognized him as the Messiah first were the Pharisees, but they did not.

Jesus shared much with the Pharisees. Indeed, as an orthodox Jew, Jesus wanted to bring the people back to an integral practice of God's law, as did the Pharisees. Like them, he was expecting the kingdom of God to come soon. Like them, he made no distinction between this coming and the restoration of Israel. Like them, he was a convinced believer in the Sabbath. He went to the temple as they did. And the Pharisee Hillel had already articulated the Golden Rule, which Jesus later reformulated.

Yet the Pharisees balked at Jesus' universal embrace. Why did they resist his revolution of social justice? Why did they refuse to heed his jubilean summons, if they really wanted to practice the Law of Moses with such great zeal?

To put it simply, the Pharisees did not repent upon hearing Jesus' call because they were offended by his requirements. They were avaricious and would not give up their exploitation of the poor. They were proud and would not abandon their prominent seats. They were authoritarian and would not allow a Galilean peasant to teach them. They were hypocrites who hid their intentions behind noble appearances.

In fact, the Pharisees felt so deeply offended by Jesus' challenge that they put the entire responsibility on Jesus. for the disagreements between them. What were their grievances? First, Jesus violated the Mosaic Law and taught others to do likewise. Moreover, Jesus did not belong to a rabbinical school and therefore had no authority to interpret the Scriptures. Jesus also threatened his nation's holiest institutions. And lastly, the political agitation Jesus created endangered the Jewish people. Let us examine each in turn.

Accusations against Jesus

The Pharisees were intent upon protecting their nation from the impure effects of hellenization. Towards this end they multiplied the ritual barriers that made mixed marriages and the mingling of peoples impossible. This was especially necessary in Galilee where the ethnic boundary lines were not as clear as they were in Judea.

The Pharisees feared corruption. They feared that the crowd that "knows nothing of the law" (John 7:49) would submerge the nucleus of faithful Israelites. The scribes, therefore, with commentaries and with commentaries on commentaries,[1] tried as conscientiously as possible to specify all possible implications of the Law of Moses. These traditions, though aimed at preserving the purity of the people, soon became more important than the Law itself.

It was these traditions Jesus attacked. The Pharisees demanded to know why Jesus allowed his disciples to break "the tradition of the elders." But Jesus had a question of his own: "And why do you break the command of God for the sake of your tradition?" The Pharisees equated the Law and tradition and so perceived in Jesus a dangerous adversary of the Law itself. But Jesus understood the issue otherwise and turned the tables around. He quoted Isaiah: "They worship me in vain; their teachings are but rules taught by men" (Matt. 15:1–9).

The Pharisees would not budge and called Jesus' authority into question. In fact, this question of authority was at the heart of the clashes between Jesus and the Pharisees. At the time, custom dictated that a rabbi, no matter how famous, should found his teaching on the commentaries of the rabbis of the preceding generation. But Jesus simply studied the Scripture. Even though he never attended a rabbinical school, he was well acquainted with the Law and the Prophets, and quoted them constantly. In fact, his first speeches stupefied his audience, because of the originality of his interpretation of the Scriptures. "He taught as one who had authority, and not as their teachers of the law" (Matt. 7:29).

Jesus drew his authority from God himself and bypassed all the rabbis, even Moses. When the scribes questioned him about the origin of his authority, Jesus refused to answer. Had he replied, "It comes from men," he would have had to show his official credentials, what today we call a university degree, which he did not have. Had he answered, "From God," his enemies could accuse him of blasphemy (Matt. 21:23–27).

So Jesus turned the question around by asking his interrogators from whom they thought John the Baptist received his authority to baptize. If they had answered, "From God," the Pharisees would be forced to change their ways. If they had answered, "John is a common man, his baptism is a fraud," the people would revolt, for they were convinced that John the Baptist was a prophet.

As good tacticians, the Pharisees did not answer him, and Jesus, for his part, also refused to answer them. Thus the question of authority remained unanswered and painfully wedged between Jesus and the Pharisees until the final drama.

Perhaps what angered the Pharisees most was Jesus' attitude toward Israel's holy institutions. Besides the temple, the religious leaders thought the Galilean prophet was questioning Israel's entire social structure—the political, ritual, and ethical institutions of the day. Every nation is inclined to equate its fundamental values with the institutional shell built to protect and express them. Consequently, its leaders are tempted to use lies to defend truth, violence to protect the peace, and persecution to save charity.

For the Pharisees the drama was even more acute because they were conscious of representing God's chosen people. They were convinced that Jesus was threatening the very foundations of Jewish identity—the institutions that were guardians of the divine absolute. When John the Baptist said, "Out of these stones God can raise up children for Abraham. The ax is already at the root of the trees…" (Matt. 3:9–10), they concluded that he was calling Israel's election into question. And when Jesus stated in the temple, "Before Abraham was born, I am!" (John 8:58), the scandal was so great that they took up stones intending to kill him.

In the Pharisees' minds, Jesus threatened not only their worldview, but even the survival of their nation. And so, when the chief priests and the Pharisees gathered in council, they showed genuine political concern. "What are we to do?" they asked themselves. "Here is this man performing many miraculous signs. If we let him go on like this, everyone will believe in him, and then the Romans will come and take away both our temple and our nation" (John 11:47–48). They truly believed that by putting an end to the young prophet's activities they were saving their people.

Yet even Pilate, though not a Jew, realized that they had delivered Jesus up because of envy. The Gospel of John reports the Pharisees saying to one another, "See, this is getting us nowhere. Look how the whole world has gone after him!" (John 12:19). Until Jesus arrived on the scene, the Pharisees' influence had met no rival.² But the miracles and speeches of Jesus were winning the people away from this influence.

Nothing is more alarming for those in power than the success of a newcomer. Besides that, Jesus was not very accommodating. A certain passage from the Sermon on the Mount concerning nonresistance to evildoers might lead one to believe that he was the passive victim of the Pharisees' plot. This was not the case. It was Jesus who began the struggle. We will now follow the stages of the conflict step by step. At each step it was Jesus who took the initiative.

Jesus Takes up the Sword

Those not familiar with the Gospels often view Jesus as the stereotypical prophet of passive nonresistance. What would happen to us, they say, if we let the wicked do as they pleased, as Jesus tells us? But to fully understand Jesus one must reexamine his words and actions as attempts to restore the original intent of the Law by destroying dehumanizing traditions. On that basis Jesus actually engaged in a kind of civil disobedience, whereby he and his disciples systematically violated those traditions that only helped to oppress the people. One by one they exposed them, and they did so with the sole aim of breaking the cast that enclosed the truth.

The events that followed the speech at Nazareth, mentioned at the beginning of this book, show how Jesus went about breaking customs that enslaved his contemporaries. We left Jesus in the synagogue when he assumed the role of Messiah. His speech was poorly received. He was too well known in his own town to begin recruiting disciples there. Those who heard him exclaimed, "Where did this man get these things? What's this wisdom that has been given him, that he even does miracles? Isn't this the carpenter? Isn't this Mary's son and the brother of James, Joses, Judas, and Simon? Aren't his sisters here with us?" So Jesus told them,

"Only in his home town, among his relatives and in his own house is a prophet without honor" (Mark 6:1–5).

The people of Nazareth dared him to perform miracles: "Do here in your home town what we have heard that you did in Capernaum." Matthew and Mark simply report that Jesus did few miracles there because of the people's lack of faith. Luke, however, gives a different explanation – Jesus did not want to perform miracles in Nazareth, and instead gave an unpatriotic speech comparing himself to Elijah and Elisha. Neither of them, he said, did any miracles in their own country because of the wickedness of their fellow countrymen (Luke 4:23–27).

Thus, Jesus completely broke with the inhabitants of Nazareth. He had attacked their pride as members of the chosen people and would suffer the consequences of his audacity. After he narrowly escaped death for the first time, he left his childhood town, never to return.

He soon broke with his family as well. At first, things were well between Jesus and his family. The Gospel of John pictures Jesus going down to Capernaum with his mother, brothers, and disciples. But this harmony did not last. Tension probably developed when Jesus started selecting his apostles. He called Simon, Andrew, James and John, but omitted his brothers. From that time on, when Mary or her sons wanted to communicate with Jesus, they had to wait outside and have an intermediary request an audience with him.

The untimely interventions of his mother and brothers had certainly made this break necessary. Jesus later said, speaking from experience, "Anyone who loves his father or mother more than me is not worthy of me" (Matt. 10:37). The day his mother wanted to see him, he asked, "Who is my mother, and who are my brothers?" This must have hurt his family very deeply. Then, pointing to his disciples, he exclaimed, "Here are my mother and my brothers.

For whoever does the will of my Father in heaven is my brother
and sister and mother" (Matt. 12:48–50). Jesus separated from his
family in order to found a new family made up of all those who
want to do God's will.

Jesus' brothers thought he had gone crazy, and so one day
some of them came to Capernaum to seize him. They found some
scribes from Jerusalem who confirmed their opinion, "He is possessed by Beelzebub! By the prince of demons he is driving out
demons" (Mark 3:22). They were convinced he was a lunatic.

Eventually, Jesus' brothers gave up trying to keep him from
acting and instead attempted to make him do imprudent things.
It is possible that some of them were Zealots and thought he was
too timid. They may have tried to accelerate the course of events
by forcing Jesus to take the leadership of a nationwide insurrection. If the uprising failed it would mean he was not the Messiah.
If it succeeded they would then join him. For this reason they
urged him to go to Judea so that his followers would see the works
he was doing. They argued, "No one who wants to become a
public figure acts in secret. Since you are doing these things, show
yourself to the world" (John 7:3–5). But Jesus did not follow their
advice and refused to go to Jerusalem at that time.

Understanding the reasons that pushed Jesus to break with his
family enables us to better understand the motives that drove him
to break with the scribes and Pharisees.

The first conflict arose over the forgiveness of sins. The
Pharisees were impressed by the healings Jesus performed. One
day, a paralytic had been let down through the roof to hear Jesus
inside. When Jesus saw his faith he said, "Friend, your sins are
forgiven" (Luke 5:20). But for the Pharisees, here Jesus had gone
too far! They were scandalized because, as they saw it, God alone
could forgive sin. In their way of thinking, there existed a kind of
accounting system between God and man, whereby only acts of
penance and offerings could absolve one from sin.

Jesus saw sin in a completely different light. It was a grave illness that attacked a person in his or her soul, much like the paralysis from which the body of the man before him was suffering. God in his loving, fatherly power wanted to restore (Matt. 9:2 uses the verb *aphiemi*) this man to spiritual wholeness, as well as to physical health. Jesus was the hand of God, the healing Messiah. He expected only one thing from the sick: faith. Whereas the Pharisees held religiously to rules and human institutions, Jesus announced an encounter between the God who "restores all things" and all those diseased in body and soul.

Another conflict arose between Jesus and the Pharisees while Jesus was recruiting apostles. The choice of the first four did not seem to have aroused any criticism. They were respectable people, fishermen on the lake, who owned their boats and their nets.

But the choice of the fifth apostle raised a wave of criticism. There was a man in Capernaum the people avoided at all costs. He was neither a leper nor a Gentile. Worse yet, he was a publican, a tax collector to whom the government had leased customs rights for the city's port, where freight from Syria was loaded onto boats. Levi had become rich and had gathered around himself a crowd of rather shady characters. His house was open to all sorts of people, his place was noisy, and those who came drank hard. This is precisely the man Jesus noticed one day sitting at the tax office. He chose him as his disciple. "Follow me!" was all Jesus said. And Levi got up, left everything and followed him (Luke 5:27–32).

Unfortunately, things did not go smoothly that night. To celebrate his new vocation, Levi invited Jesus and his disciples to a feast. Levi's friends joined them. They began to eat and drink. Now, the whole city knew the reputation of Levi's friends. The scribes from among the Pharisees motioned for some of Jesus' disciples to come out. They still had some regard for the prophet of Nazareth and they wanted to help him out of a scrape. "Why does your teacher eat with tax collectors and 'sinners'?" they asked (Matt. 9:11).

Jesus overheard them and responded that he enjoyed being around publicans and sinners, not to adopt their lifestyle, but because they were sick and in need. He asked: Is the doctor reproached for his contacts with sick people? Then why would anyone want me to turn away from those who need me most? Is it for fear of catching some ritual impurity or for fear of public opinion? I have come for those who are poor in soul and body. They are looking for me, but you, who consider yourselves and your practices healthy, refuse to see your need. And since you think you don't need me, I have not come to you. My kingdom is only for those who want to be healed (Matt. 9:12–13).

The Pharisees and even the disciples of John the Baptist were annoyed that Jesus and his disciples never fasted. Instead of displaying the appropriate austerity, they must have formed a joyous group. One can imagine them going through the streets of the Galilean cities, chatting and joking, in no way affecting the stern expressions on the faces of the Pharisees and John's disciples. When asked why, Jesus turned the question around: Why is it that my disciples do not fast? Ask me, rather, why they should fast at all. Is there anything sad about the kingdom of God? They are on the way to a wedding banquet with the bridegroom. In the name of what ill-natured spirit do you want to prevent the bridegroom's companions from rejoicing? (Luke 5:33–35).

Yet another conflict between Jesus and the Pharisees had to do with the Sabbath. In this case, Jesus deliberately and visibly demonstrated his opposition. The Jews were forbidden to do any work on the Sabbath. In particular, they could not harvest, thresh, winnow, glean the harvest, grind the grain, or carry food from one house to another. All Jews, except the most rebellious, kept the Sabbath holy. Anyone who violated it was required to go to Jerusalem and offer a special sacrifice.

But on one Sabbath day Jesus passed through a ripe grain field. With his consent, his disciples tore off the heads of grain, rubbed them in their hands, and ate them. By doing this, they were simultaneously violating all six of the legal prescriptions mentioned above! The Pharisees were shocked "Look! Your disciples are doing what is unlawful on the Sabbath" (Matt. 12:1–2).

Jesus' response to the Pharisees is most revealing: You criticize my disciples for eating when they are hungry? What was the purpose behind the Sabbath in the first place? Do you think God created us to be bound by a thousand and one sabbatical ordinances? Is the Sabbath God's punishment in order to torture human beings? No! "The Sabbath was made for man, not man for the Sabbath" (Mark 2:27). It is a day of liberation, a gift from God that we may rest.[3]

Since his adversaries still insisted, Jesus cut the controversy short by a final argument. He reminded them that when David was hungry he did not hesitate to break the law by eating the consecrated bread in the temple, which was only for priests. Besides, Jesus told them that, as the Son of Man announced by the prophets, he is greater than the temple. He is even master of the Sabbath (Matt. 12:3–8).

Why was it so important for Jesus to defy his contemporaries, to associate with shady characters, to adopt easygoing manners, to dissociate himself from pious folk, and to authorize his disciples to violate the Sabbath? Was it really necessary for him, by irritating Jewish opinions on mere details, to jeopardize the success of his gigantic undertaking, the establishment of God's kingdom? Would it not have been wiser for him, who wanted to give the Sabbath its original meaning, to conform temporarily to the accepted customs, gain a good, serious reputation, and then try to reform the institutions of Judaism from the inside?

The best explanation may be that Jesus had the soul of a revolutionary. He had come, he said, to create something brand-new, from the bottom up: Do you think I will tear the new garment of my teaching in order to patch the worn-out robe of your old practices? Certainly not! The new patch would tear the old cloth and make the hole worse, and my new garment would also be ruined. And this wine of my kingdom, filled with ferment, do you think I will pour it into the old wineskins of your traditions? Of course not! My teaching would burst your customs. The wine would spill and be lost as well as your wineskins. Pour new wine into new wineskins, and both are preserved.[4]

Jesus' message was unequivocal. He came not only to change individuals but to restore God's people. He had to change practices as well as hearts in order to restore God's justice in the world. If institutions were not changed, if conventions were not challenged, they would smother under their weight the noblest souls – even those who had been momentarily awakened to his call for a better world. And if Jesus did not hesitate to defy conventions, neither should we!

These confrontations with the Pharisees reveal the nature of the "sword" Jesus wielded. His sharpness and defiance were necessary to cut people – and even institutions – free from the stifling cast of human tradition.

Yet Jesus' revolution was always fueled by an overwhelming compassion. This was the profound motive that impelled him to restore God's covenant with his people to its original purity. He was not anti-establishment, per se. He came not to condemn, but as a physician to heal and restore. God is love. He wants human beings, bearers of his image, to be treated with respect and mercy. This is why the Messiah risked losing his life at the hands of tradition's defenders in order to heal the sick, the weak, and the least of his brothers.

CHAPTER THIRTEEN

Nonviolent Love and the Person

Jesus overturned the Jewish institutions of his day because the cast of human traditions had to be broken. The truth had to be set free so that Israel's election could become available to all nations. Jesus' conflict with the guardians of the Jewish institutions was so acute that, humanly seen, it would appear he was faced with only two options: war – with the Pharisees first, then with the Romans, which would have greatly pleased the Zealots – or withdrawal from the world, which would have greatly pleased religious purists such as the Essenes.

Jesus, however, chose a third path: the nonviolent entry as Messiah into Jerusalem, his capital city. More than a "triumphal entry," Jesus' nonviolent option was packed with redemptive significance. His sacrifice would be the supreme mark of divine compassion. But nonviolence was merely the framework. In this chapter, we will attempt to discover more precisely the content Jesus wanted to give his nonviolent action.

Redemptive Nonviolence

Though Jesus had given up violence, he did so without abandoning the struggle for liberation. He would be crucified and yet rise victoriously. We will not go into all the reasons for Jesus' death. Jesus himself was extremely reserved on the subject, and the Gospels contain practically no "theology" of the crucifixion! The first three are very sparing in their comments. Jesus invites his disciples to follow him: "If anyone would come after me, he must deny himself and take up his cross and follow me"(Matt. 16:24). The cross, not the way of violence, would be the sign of the kingdom of God. It was not meant for the Redeemer alone. Every disciple is a "cross-bearer."

Elsewhere Jesus claimed to be a "ransom," and explained what this would require of his followers: "You know that those who are regarded as rulers of the Gentiles lord it over them, and their high officials exercise authority over them. Not so with you. Instead, whoever wants to become great among you must be your servant, and whoever wants to be first must be slave of all. For even the Son of Man did not come to be served, but to serve, and to give his life as a ransom for many" (Mark 10:42–45). What does "being a ransom" entail? It demands serving others to the point of losing one's life, like the good shepherd in John 10:1–21. And it involves exchanging one's life for the life of a prisoner, like the *goel* of the Old Testament.

Quoting from the prophet Isaiah, the Gospel of Matthew equates Jesus' healing of sickness and sin to the actions of the *goel*, the Servant of the Lord: "When evening came…he drove out the spirits with a word and healed all the sick. This was to fulfill what was spoken through the prophet Isaiah: 'He took up our infirmities and carried our diseases'" (Matt. 8:16–17). This passage is well worth quoting in its entirety because it can shed some light on the profundity of Jesus' thought. "Surely he took up our infirmities and carried our sorrows, yet we considered him stricken by God, smitten by him, and afflicted. But he was pierced for our transgressions, he was crushed by our iniquities; the punishment that

brought us peace was upon him, and by his wounds we are healed"
(Isa. 53:4–5).

Taking into account the Old Testament references to the
Redeemer's role, we should take a closer look at an exception-
ally important event, again concerning the Sabbath, which took
place in the synagogue at Capernaum. According to Luke, this
event took place after the series of clashes described in the previous chapter, which had been provoked by the proclamation of the
Jubilee and had put Jesus on the verge of a violent conflict with
the Pharisees.

> On another Sabbath Jesus went into the synagogue and was teach-
> ing, and a man was there whose right hand was shriveled. The
> Pharisees and the teachers of the law were looking for a reason to
> accuse Jesus, so they watched him closely to see if he would heal
> on the Sabbath. But Jesus knew what they were thinking and said
> to the man with the shriveled hand, "Get up and stand in front of
> everyone." So he got up and stood there.
>
> Then Jesus said to them, "I ask you, which is lawful on the
> Sabbath: to do good or to do evil, to save life or to destroy it?"
>
> He looked around at them all, and then said to the man,
> "Stretch out your hand." He did so, and his hand was completely
> restored. But they were furious and began to discuss with one
> another what they might do to Jesus. (Luke 6:1–11)[2]

The young prophet's popularity was so great in Capernaum that the
Pharisees felt they were being supplanted in their own synagogue.
It was customary on the Sabbath for a distinguished guest to be
invited to read the Scripture and comment upon it. On this particular Sabbath, Jesus himself seems to have led the service. Irritated
and jealous as the Pharisees were, they decided to keep Jesus from
making the people stray from their healthy religious observances.
They had probably contacted Herod's police to prepare for the
prophet's arrest (Mark 3:6). These proud adversaries of Hellenism
and Antipas had stooped rather low by requesting the intervention of their worst enemies, the Herodians!

The scribes and Pharisees in the audience were watching Jesus attentively. They hoped to catch him in the act of breaking the law, and then have him indicted and condemned to death. Jesus was perfectly aware of this. There was still time for him to either take up arms or withdraw from the struggle by avoiding a confrontation with his adversaries. Reformers at every historical turning point seem forced to choose the "lesser of two evils" – war or resignation. Jesus, however, would find a third way and thus eliminate this merciless false dilemma for all his disciples.

Notice first that Jesus' attention was focused on a human being, a man with a withered hand. Still today, when the problem of the "lesser evil" is discussed,[3] the human being as an individual is almost always overlooked. People argue, "Our nation is about to be exterminated; or the future of our civilization, of our moral values, of true religion is threatened; or yet, our institutions violate human rights, and to save human rights we must suspend our scruples and use violence, sacrificing human lives to destroy unjust structures, and thus saving the poor from oppression."

Today's revolutionaries assert, "The misery of the hungry is so deep, the liberation of the exploited so urgent and the requirements of justice so exacting, that we are forced to choose violence rather than resignation; the sacrifice of millions today is preparing for a better tomorrow." For centuries both progressive and reactionary camps have been "temporarily" choosing violence, "temporarily" shedding the blood of millions of victims in the name of a better future.[4] Because each side speculates about "what would happen if we let our enemy win," they mercilessly sacrifice the individual, whether friend or enemy, this common man whom Jesus referred to as our neighbor.

Every generation, it seems, feels compelled at one point or another to use violence. Once the crisis has passed, the following generation is unable to appreciate the climate that engendered such wars. We are already incapable of imagining the collective emotions that led to the war of succession in Spain, or the Crimean War, or World War 1.⁵ It is all the harder for us to imagine what the problems of Hellenism, of Roman occupation, or of the preservation versus the rejection of traditional Sabbath forms meant for Jesus. However, if one considers that today's struggles for democratic freedom, for national independence, for the abolition of colonialism, or for social justice are extremely important, how much more important the struggle for the kingdom of God must have seemed to Jesus. He undoubtedly saw it as the ultimate struggle of history.

The seriousness of the situation could have caused Jesus to "temporarily" forget the plight of this man with his withered hand in the synagogue. His name was not preserved. The people of Capernaum were probably used to him being around. He was quite likely one of those unimportant poor people who begged at the doors of religious gatherings, a man who was unable to work because of the condition of his hand. The Gospel does not even tell us that he asked to be healed. He was simply sitting there.

As Jesus was speaking, he could have glanced over the audience and ignored that withered hand. But the Messiah would not let traditions or institutions or righteous causes blind us to the need of our neighbor. He wanted to break the bars of the religious prison of his day, the prison of the status quo where those in power ignore those without, and the opportunity before him was exceptional. He knew his action might lead to his own arrest and death, but this was no objection. Jesus would not back down or turn back. Let the tyranny of social indifference, of self-righteous piety perish – and with it his own chances of success! A new justice had to prevail. This totally new justice would be founded upon the ransom that Jesus was going to pay for the life of a man.

Jesus told the disabled man to stand up. He wanted everyone to see what was about to happen. Why didn't he avoid the scandal at the last moment? Why didn't he whisper in the man's ear, "As you can see, the circumstances are not very favorable today. Come and see me tomorrow morning at Simon Peter's house and I will heal you"? Had not the sick man been waiting for years? Could he not wait one day longer? No! Jesus wanted to act on the spot not only because of his sabbatical revolution, but also in the name of something more important. The man stood before Jesus, and Jesus said, "Stretch out your hand." The man stretched out his hand and it was completely restored.

On that day, voluntarily, officially, in a Jewish "church," before numerous witnesses, Jesus violated the rabbinical traditions that regulated the Sabbath, a crime deserving the death penalty.[6] And so the scribes and the Pharisees immediately left and made a complaint to Herod's police. Justice was to follow its course, the complaint would reach Jerusalem, and several months later, the criminal would be executed.

What drove Jesus to do this? For what reason, or better, for whom, did Jesus do this deed of goodness? The one for whom Jesus had sacrificed everything was standing in the middle of the synagogue. Who was he? An important figure on whom the future of humanity depended? No, he was only a man, a "common man," whom Jesus had taken out of his anonymity and placed at the center, and for whom he had "exchanged" his life.

Who was this poor man's *goel?* Who was the brother or the cousin offering himself voluntarily as a ransom for him? Was he the anonymous soldier in Yahweh's army, the one everyone gladly sacrifices for a noble cause? No! He was the central figure of human history, God's Messiah, who had come with the prodigious task of establishing God's kingdom on earth.

Thus Jesus demonstrated God's answer for Israel. His way was no moral theory. Redemption was not some metaphysical idea.

The power of redemption took place on a specific day in human history. One person was saved; another risked his own life. Jesus was the *goel* who redeemed the man with the withered hand by forsaking his glorious position for a miserable destiny.

Foundations of Nonviolence

Jesus' entire career was a succession of redemptive acts such as the one at Capernaum, and they all led to the cross. This is Jesus' third way: a nonviolent love that commits itself to the redemption of the individual person. This primary preoccupation outweighed his respect for the Law and the temple, as well as the urgency of a religious, social, and political revolution. It even preempted the immediate establishment of the kingdom of God on earth. This one preoccupation was the lot of a single human being, the healing of a sick hand!

This does not mean Jesus gave up his revolution. Unlike most revolutionaries, who deviate from their primary aim out of concern for efficiency, Jesus remained focused on the plight of individual human beings, and by so doing gave his kingdom an importance like no other political movement before or since. A new civilization would grow out of it. However, to limit Christianity to a gospel of individual salvation would betray Jesus. The individual who is redeemed by his *goel*, Christ, is also the material for a new religious, social, and political fabric willed by God.

At Capernaum Jesus explained to his furious or marveling listeners why he violated the Sabbath. First, he asked, "Which is lawful on the Sabbath: to do good or to do evil, to save life or to destroy it?" With these words, Jesus clearly exposed the problem with all institutions. He was not abolishing the Sabbath. Rather, he was justifying it: "The Sabbath was made for man." But on the pretense of protecting the people from the corruption of the Gentiles, the Sabbath had become a means of enslaving them to inhuman rules and practices. Jesus was simply reminding the people that the Sabbath – and other institutions for that matter – had no other purpose than to do them good. The Sabbath and the Year of Jubilee were meant to reestablish justice and give the weak their place in society.

Precisely because it was a Sabbath day, the Messiah had to do good on that day. Good could not wait to be done. To put it off would have been a crime.[7] The Sabbath is there to do God's will. This is the day that the suffering person must be made whole.

People tend to think of nonviolence as a choice between using force and doing nothing. But for Jesus, the real choice takes place at another level. Nonviolence is less a matter of "not killing" and more a matter of showing compassion, of saving and redeeming, of being a healing community. One must choose between doing good to the person placed in one's path, or the evil which one might be doing by mere abstention. For Jesus, there is no no-man's-land, enabling us to portion our attitudes, to do a little good to our neighbor without taking the risk of becoming involved for his sake, or to do him a little harm while still remaining charitable.

In the synagogue, Jesus had to choose between good and evil done to a neighbor. He refused to measure the far-off consequences of his action. His explanation is in no way obscure. To do good is to save a person; not to do him good is to kill him. To save someone is to restore that person physically, socially, and spiritually. To neglect and postpone this restoration is already to kill.

Although the man with the withered hand was not in danger of losing his life, Jesus could not neglect him. He had come to save the entire person, and that immediately. Elsewhere in the Gospels, as in this case, Jesus made no distinction between body and soul. To save is to heal at once the entire human being, body and soul. To kill is to destroy the entire human being, body and soul. One cannot kill the body to save the soul, or kill the soul to save the body. The well-known words: "Whoever tries to keep his life will lose it, but whoever loses his life will preserve it," do not mean that one can save one's soul by hurling one's body into death. It is not the sacrifice of the body that counts, but the unlimited dedication of our entire being, body and soul, to a cause more important than our life. The cause Jesus proposed is a person – himself. The cause for which he gave his own life is also a person – you. His revolution was a genuinely human one; people, not principles, were his concern.

To make his point crystal clear, Jesus appealed to conscience and to rustic common sense: "If any of you has a sheep and it falls into a pit on the Sabbath, will you not take hold of it and lift it out?" (Matt. 12:11–12). Everyone who has lived on a farm knows that cattle cannot go without eating or drinking on Sunday. Every peasant, no matter how pious, is tied down by his duties toward his animals. Even the Pharisees themselves, who were sometimes farmers, took care of their cattle on the Sabbath.[8] No ritual prescription could oppose a requirement of this type.

But Jesus went one step further. The peasant of his example owns only one sheep. We find here the framework of the parable of the good shepherd for whom his one lost sheep is worth as much as the ninety-nine safe ones. But in this case, the shepherd owns only this one sheep. In the synagogue, Jesus looked at the beggar with his hand and saw him with the eyes of a God who would only possess one man in the world. God's love centers totally on each person as if he or she were the only one.

Jesus, the Messiah, the arm of God, has only one sheep. It is his only wealth. But this sheep is wounded; it has fallen into an abandoned pit. Jesus appealed to the hearts of his listeners. You who own only one sheep, would you let it die because it is the Sabbath? Of course not! That would not be in your interest, and your kindness would also prompt you to save it. The Sabbath does not oppose these things. And turning to the Pharisees, he said, "How much more valuable is a man than a sheep!"

On that Sabbath day, in a small synagogue at Capernaum, Jesus showed that in God's eyes each person is unique and comes before anything else. To restore our sacredness, the sacrosanct tradition will be violated, the Messiah will be condemned to death, and he will rise again. The kingdom of God will take a different form, for the future will center on the newborn child of history: the person.

The Costly Way

We have seen that nonviolence was integral to Jesus' teachings. But nonviolence toward whom? In the synagogue of Capernaum, Jesus gave an object and a body to his ethical teaching, namely, our neighbor, the person in need. It was also on that day that Jesus laid the indestructible foundations of Christian nonviolence, by limiting his disciples to the only true dilemma worth considering. The choice is not between violence or withdrawal, but between doing good or doing harm, that is, to save or to kill.[9]

By choosing to save at the cost of his life, Jesus forever joined two realities: redemption and nonviolence. Because Jesus is the Redeemer, no one can any longer save by killing or kill to save. Life alone, life given, not life exacted from others, can save life.

Because Jesus was ready to give his life as a ransom for humanity, he did not require his disciples to sacrifice themselves then and there. He certainly saw that they would die as martyrs (Mark 10:39), but only at the time God would choose. He was giving his life so that his disciples might live: "While I was with them, I protected them and…none has been lost…" (John 17:12). Shortly after speaking these words, Jesus was arrested in the Garden of Gethsemane. The Roman cohort and the temple officer said they were looking for Jesus of Nazareth. Jesus answered, "I told you that I am he…If you are looking for me, then let these men go." And the writer added: "This happened so that the words he had spoken would be fulfilled: 'I have not lost one of those you gave me'" (John 18:7–9). Clearly, then, when Jesus used the words "to lose" and "to save," he meant both the physical and the spiritual life of his disciples.

The deep personal love Jesus showed in caring for his disciples and his mother to the very end rids the passion story of any false heroism.[10] His love for them is matched only by his care for the crowd that lamented him: "Daughters of Jerusalem, do not weep for me; weep for yourselves and for your children." For a man who came to arrest him: he healed his ear. For his companion of execution: "I tell you the truth, today you will be with me in paradise." And even for those who were crucifying him: "Father, forgive them, for they do not know what they are doing."[11]

By demonstrating a genuinely different heroism, a personal and self-sacrificing love, Jesus invalidated any argument in favor of a Christian heroism that would manifest itself in the bloody solidarity of battlefields. In his own words, "Greater love has no one than this, that he lay down his life for his friends" (John 15:13).

CHAPTER FOURTEEN

The Greatest Commandment

For the time being, until the Last Judgment, the throne of vengeance is unoccupied. In the place of the avenging God there is the Lamb of God, the *goel* who takes away the sin of the world. Yes, *of the world.*

None of us is capable of doing good, at least not without dirty hands. It is downright dangerous to try to justify ourselves, for doing so puts us in the place of God. A moralizing religion, a religion of works, even of nonviolence, only raises the screen of pride between us and God, and between us and others. What, then, remains to guide our conduct? What can compel us toward a new future? What is at the heart of Jesus' nonviolent revolution? *A loving respect for our neighbor, the person right before us.*

A New Command

Jesus sums up in two sentences the entire Mosaic Law and the Prophets, that is, the duty of holiness and of prophetic mission in the world: "Love the Lord your God with all your heart and with all your soul and with all your mind and with all your strength; and love your neighbor as yourself. There is no commandment greater than these" (Mark 12:30–31). Although these two commands are found in the Old Testament, what is original in Jesus' teaching is that he brings them together. They become a singular command. Jesus is saying that we cannot love God if we do not love our brother; God will not forgive us if we do not forgive our brother (Matt. 6:14–15). In short, we shall be judged as we judge others.

Why is Jesus so rigid on this point? Because anyone who sets limits toward loving his neighbor raises a wall between himself and the God whose love knows no limits. God's kingdom seeks to overcome barriers. This is why Jesus is extraordinarily indulgent toward sinners. He displays unbounded love and kindness toward them; he never ceases to believe in the possibility of their turning from their sin. But he is uncompromising with hypocrites, that is, with the spiritually proud who have no love for their brothers and sisters.[1]

Jesus' new commandment demands that we translate the rulership of God into everyday language through our bodies: Love your neighbor, serve him, heal him, even if this means breaking traditions or laws. Give in to him rather than offend him and turn him away from God. Whatever you do, don't make yourself an obstacle on his way to God. One's neighbor's physical wellbeing is as important as his spiritual life; the healing of the body and the healing of the soul are joined in a single operation.[2] Christ's revolution is total, or it is nothing.

The immediacy and simplicity of this new commandment liberate us from fears, from plans, from complicated orders issued by the state, whether in peacetime or in wartime, and from all that divides people from one another. Freed from all casuistry, one can joyfully serve others as well as refuse with the same joy any attempt on humanity's existence. We no longer need to be impressed by great principles quoted to us, or with great historical moments that call for bloodshed. It is so simple. Any endeavor to serve the needs of others, especially those that benefit children, the persecuted, prisoners, the exploited, the aged, the infirm, will advance God's kingdom, even if only minutely.

The Christian objector to war or military service is thus not a purist who, on the day he receives orders to kill his neighbor, wakes from his dream to say no.[3] He is a servant with experienced hands, who is so busy helping his neighbor that to interrupt his activity to undertake the task of killing is unthinkable to him.

Perhaps it is true that certain violent remedies employed against tyrants have put an end to certain forms of evil, but they have not eliminated evil. Evil itself will take root elsewhere, as we have seen through history. The fertilizer that stimulates its growth is yesterday's violence. Even "just wars" and "legitimate defense" bring vengeance in their train. Fresh crimes invariably ensue.[4]

But the future of the person who turns to God is not determined by the past, and therefore neither is the future of humanity. God's forgiveness creates the possibility of an entirely new future. The cross breaks the cycle of violence. The sacrifice of Jesus opens an un-expected way to possibilities that are constantly renewed. This is why yesterday's conscientious objector, yesterday's resister, is never truly satisfied. He is troubled because he has not been able to make a visible contribution to the checking of evil, and because indirectly his own hands are stained with his neighbor's blood. Will he then resign himself next time to taking up arms? By no means. God will open doors to him that now seem shut.[5]

The state—the way of power—can only work from the past to anticipate the future and determine its course. As long as the church abandons its calling, the state will know nothing of repentance. But the church in its midst *does* know repentance, and it knows only that, and it bears witness to that before the state, for the healing of the nations. If Christ's followers do not surpass the state in justice, they do not belong to God's kingdom; they leave the world to fend for itself in the agony of its abandonment.[6]

Meanwhile Jesus, even if deserted by his church, climbs the road to Calvary, continuing to seek and to save those that are lost.

Loving One's Enemy

In addition to the lost and rejected there is the "enemy." Christians have been and continue to be divided over the meaning of Jesus' words, "You have heard that it was said, 'Eye for eye, and tooth for tooth.' But I tell you, do not resist[7] an evil person. If someone strikes you on the right cheek, turn to him the other also" (Matt. 5:38–39). The minority view has been: "These words are categorical; we must put them into practice, whatever the cost." But the majority answers: "Jesus is expressing himself in paradoxes. Experience shows that the power of the wicked is too great on earth. Sometimes one must resist them with weapons. If everyone gave his coat to the robber who demands it, the order that God wants in the world would be lost. We must help the state preserve God's order."

The majority is right insofar as nonviolence must never be made into an article of law, or into some ethical imperative apart from faith. Nonviolence can only overcome evil if it is the act of God's power on earth, working through human beings. If living nonviolently amounts to passivity, it may even encourage evil. But the majority is wrong if it accuses pacifists of wanting to keep their hands clean. Nonviolence engages evil, it does not withdraw from it.

The coming of Mahatma Gandhi, whose life and teaching surprisingly resemble those of Jesus, revived the whole issue of nonviolence just when majority theology thought it had already answered the question negatively.

This is not to say that Gandhi's teaching is the same as Jesus'. The way of nonviolent love is not some common denominator that all the great religions share, and it is a mistake for a disciple of Jesus to venerate Gandhi as much as Christ, or to seek a universal religion where all conflicting viewpoints would be reconciled. In reacting against such syncretism, official Christian theology has, unfortunately, discarded Gandhi. It dismisses a nonviolence whose roots, it claims, are not Christian. (As we have seen, nonviolence has roots not only in Jesus' action but also in the Old Testament.)

However, if Christians discount loving one's enemies on account of its impracticality, then they need to look again at Gandhi's witness – both in terms of similarities and differences.

Gandhi, like Jesus, belonged to a nation oppressed for several generations by a foreign power. The British, like the Romans, used the old method of dividing in order to rule, perpetuated old quarrels between princes and provinces, and either instated or overthrew the docile petty kings whenever they needed to do so. In India there were collaborators, as there were among the Jews in Jesus' days, who adopted their master's culture to the point of forgetting their own language. But there were also patriots who found in their religion and in their national traditions a burning thirst for independence. The British, like the Romans, generally showed themselves tolerant toward local custom and worship as long as these did not disturb the peace. Armed revolts sprang up in India, as in Palestine, but they were promptly crushed.

Thus Gandhi, like Jesus, lived among collaborators, as well as among partisans in a war of independence. Both Gandhi and Jesus could have sheltered themselves in a spiritual cloister. Instead, they opened the way to a new kind of freedom.

Both men stressed the moral and spiritual conditions of liberation. Both demanded more from themselves than from their disciples, more from their disciples than from their people, more from their people than from their adversaries. Both were men of prayer. Neither ever bound his message to the political platform of a particular party, choosing instead to remain on the sidelines as an inspirator and counselor for everyone. They both sent messages to cities and towns to proclaim repentance, a radical change in the way of life, the end of social injustice, and the abolition of a hypocritical caste system. Their violent deaths show a final similarity. Gandhi, like Jesus, died blessing his assassins.

But here the analogy stops. Gandhi had a political aim. He wanted to unify his people and liberate them from the foreign yoke. To reach his goal, he used only *satyagraha* (the power of truth), and put it to work through *ahimsa* (nonviolence). After twenty-five years of struggle, he reached his goal and obtained national independence. From a human standpoint, he succeeded.

From a human standpoint, Jesus failed. Moreover, his aim was not the same as Gandhi's. His goal was never merely the national liberation of Israel. He wanted to prepare, then inaugurate the kingdom of God on earth. His nonviolence was not a means to reach this end,[8] but rather a matter of obedience and witness to God, who is love and who alone will establish his kingdom on earth. Like the Jewish prophets before him, Jesus knew that national liberation would never come so long as God's people were unfaithful. And because they were unfaithful, God would call together a universal people, formed by all those who answer God's call. In the end, Jesus' failure on the national level transformed his mission into a universal one.

Another difference between Gandhi and Jesus is that Gandhi understood the command "turn the other cheek" as a maneuver in a game of chess.

> Nonviolence is not a resignation from all real fighting against wickedness. On the contrary, the nonviolence of my conception is a more active and real fight against wickedness than retaliation, whose very nature is to increase wickedness…I seek entirely to blunt the edge of the tyrant's sword, not by putting up against it a sharper-edged weapon, but by disappointing his expectation that I would be offering physical resistance. The resistance of the soul that I should offer would elude him. I would at first dazzle him and

at last compel recognition from him, which would not humiliate but uplift him.[9]

In short, Gandhi accepted the challenge of the enemy because he knew he was a better player and would eventually win. This fundamental optimism did not lead him astray. His nonviolence stimulated the energies of the Indian people, which finally overcame British colonialism. From a more general standpoint, Gandhi showed that the Sermon on the Mount can, in many circumstances, be politically effective.[10] The demonstration of such effectiveness in the age of technology and nuclear weapons is one of the great moral victories of the twentieth century.

To claim that Jesus in the Sermon on the Mount was proposing a Gandhian-type "chess game," however, is to distort his message. Jesus certainly did not give up the possibility of changing his enemies' hearts, but the motive for his nonviolence is elsewhere, namely in God himself, a God who for centuries has dealt with a thankless people, and who has continuously shown his love for the good and the wicked alike by sending sun and rain. To be "sons of the Most High" (Luke 6:35), we must be loving, and therefore nonviolent, without hoping to necessarily overcome or overpower anybody.

Jesus stated, "Blessed are those who are persecuted because of righteousness," without promising any earthly successes other than the final coming of God's kingdom. In the same line of thought, he later said, "If anyone would come after me, he must deny himself and take up his cross and follow me." This self-denial to which Jesus referred is not the ascetic discipline Gandhi prescribed for his disciples to prepare them for nonviolent combat,[11] but something far deeper. It is a preparation for the possible failure of their attempts and for physical death, when the enemy will think he is the victor. God alone will change the cross into a victory.

One should not, however, exaggerate the gospel's pessimism. In Jesus' mind, God always triumphs eventually, and he triumphs immediately wherever faith is found on earth among people of good will. But the final victory comes after, not before, the cross. One could say that Jesus sees nonviolence as inseparable from small groups of people of faith, who live by God's grace and whose purpose on earth is to be God's witnesses of redemption. These groups are the salt of the earth, the light of the world, the city on a hill.

The Reality of Evil

In his autobiography Gandhi tells how he tried as sincerely as possible to acquire faith in Christ as his Savior. But the bloody struggle fought by God in his son on the cross was incomprehensible to him. His Hindu mind saw evil, as well as good, as a manifestation of divinity. It is therefore useless to combat evil.

In other words, Gandhi did not believe in the reality of evil outside himself. Evil was in himself as a consequence of his own ignorance, his own desires, his own egoism. Had he overcome these inner obstacles and dissipated these illusions, the problem of external evil would no longer exist. This is the Hindu doctrine. So Gandhi projected onto the world his optimistic views about evil as an inner illusion that contemplation can dissipate. On the contrary, for Jesus, who was free from the problems of personal sin, evil was an objective reality, outside himself, that should be fought with utmost energy.[12]

Hindu nonviolence stems from a belief in the illusory character of all appearances, even the transitory appearance of the human being with his suffering. Christian nonviolence, on the contrary, grows out of the unique worth of each human being in God's sight. "Why kill the evildoer?" asks the Hindu. "It will merely hasten his reincarnation. Violence is useless and aberrant.

It belongs to the world of illusory passions that delay the return of all beings to God." By contrast, the Christian argues, "I cannot kill the evildoer. By shortening his earthly life, I am running the risk of taking away an opportunity for him to repent and be reconciled with God." God is patient, not wishing that any should perish.[13]

"God," says Gandhi, "is continuously acting; He never rests… However, his tireless activity is the only true rest." Jesus also found his rest in God. He withdrew to be near to God in solitude, to regain strength through prayer, and to prepare for action. But the God of Jesus is a personal and acting God. He is the God of the Jewish prophets, who cannot rest as long as the scandal of sin and death lasts. From this tension between the God of justice who requires the destruction of sin and the punishment of the guilty, and the God of love who does not want the least of his children to perish – from this contradiction sprang redemption.

This redemption is not a vague concept, but an action that happened in time, a unique event that marked a date in the history of humanity. From a Hindu perspective time is illusory; everything is already accomplished in God. From a Christian perspective, however, time is real. There was a period before redemption, a time of struggle between God's love and justice. Then there was an hour of decision when God's justice and love were reconciled by Jesus' sacrifice on the cross. And now we live in an "in-between time" conditioned by Christ's redemptive act and placed under the responsibility of those who obey God's call until the coming of the Messiah's reign.

By deriving nonviolence not from a philosophy of the universe (which may be utopian), but from his sacrifice on the cross, Jesus gives it historical precision and a much greater impact. Repentance is necessary, forgiveness is real. Through redemption, nonviolence thrusts itself on all Jesus' disciples. It becomes an article of faith, a mark of obedience, a sign of the kingdom to come.

However, the differences between Jesus and Gandhi should not be carried to an extreme. Gandhi also saw nonviolence as unconditional obedience to God, who is truth and love.

> You have asked me why I consider that God is Truth…I would say with those who say God is Love: "God is Love." But deep down in me I used to say that though God may be God, God is Truth above all. I have come to the conclusion that for myself God is Truth, but two years ago I went a step further and said Truth is God. And I came to that conclusion after a continuous and relentless search after Truth, which began nearly fifty years ago. I then found that the nearest approach to Truth was through Love.[14]

Beyond Compromise

Though Gandhi failed to grasp God's redemptive plan in Christ, Christians should be exceedingly thankful for the "ethical revolution of the twentieth century" he initiated.[15] Gandhi has shown that what Jesus taught in the Sermon on the Mount works. The arguments of those who have tried to prove that Jesus' ethic was not made for this earth, or that it was reserved for a select few, have been debunked. Loving one's enemy can be applied to the town square and to the battlefield. If it is relevant there, it has all the more relevance for private life.

Why then do today's Christians hesitate to put Jesus' love-command into practice? The reason is that Christians, especially in the West, participate in the power structure. Their ethic is one of "realism." It is one of compromise with honors, power, money, and war, and they cannot free themselves from it.[16] "We are putting the doctrine of grace through faith into practice," they say, "not grace through works. The apostle Paul is our master." Are they so sure Paul would claim them as his own? The grace Paul preached is given to those who, like him, have tried to obey God in all things by patterning their lives after Christ. It is only on account of their courageous struggle that Paul tells them that it is faith that saves, not inner or outward success.[17]

What can God say to those who have given up following Christ before even starting, or who have settled down in a comfortable mediocrity? Grace will never reach these people, because they don't really need grace to gain their salvation. Theirs is a salvation through compromise.

Perhaps if the teachings of Gandhi prevailed in the church, Christians would once again see their need and sin; they would truly repent and the power of divine grace would really come over them. When the church turns its back on the way of Jesus, its ethical teaching is lost in the intricacies of mediocre casuistry and its members fall into pharasaic moralism.

Of course, one can err in the opposite direction. Nonviolence can become a fad, and has in some circles. It can be reduced to a cluster of techniques, vivisected from the greater vision. These techniques, of course, should not be ignored. After all, they can be used to obtain good results. But one can too easily forget that Christ-like nonviolence is rooted in love, and is therefore above all a witness to God. Should nonviolence become merely a method by which to "gain the whole world," just another type of force, it would quickly be used for political ends of dubious integrity. And then what would be left of it?

Christians must remember that evil is no illusion. Evil cannot be eliminated by inner discipline alone or by silent demonstrations. God himself could not economize on redemption. Are we stronger than God? Have we found a cure-all that would allow us to bypass the cross of Christ? Gandhi, who did not understand redemption, knew he was a sinner and bemoaned the imperfection of his deeds. He was cut to the heart when the liberation of India coincided with bloody struggles between Hindus and

Muslims and finally resulted in the schism of the country. Should Christians be more superficial than Gandhi?

If history is dominated by two events that unfold in time – the redemption accomplished by Christ on the cross, and the final coming of the kingdom of God – then Gandhi's accomplishment and others like it must be viewed as premonitory signs of the kingdom. Through them we are all called to repentance, to renewed faith in the God of redemption, and to hope in the final victory of Christ.

Followers of Christ must therefore put aside their excuses and agonize over their failure to love. But in doing so there is hope. Jesus brought a new commandment precisely because he brought with him a new possibility. The future he promised awaits those who are willing to take hold of it.

CHAPTER FIFTEEN

The Politics of Witness

B efore we conclude our study, we must determine how Jesus himself related to the state, and how he wanted his followers to act toward the government.

As we have seen, in Jesus' time two authorities represented the state: the Jewish authority, theocratic in type, consisting of the Sanhedrin in Jerusalem; and the occupying authority, in the person of the Roman procurator. Jesus addressed himself to each of these on several occasions. He never associated himself with their activities, nor did his disciples. Nor did Peter, Paul, or John ever make the slightest allusion to any sort of collaboration. Their attitude toward the civil authorities was nonviolent in the best sense of the word. They acted prophetically, uttering warnings and pronouncing severe judgments against the state, yet never inciting armed revolt.

According to Jesus, the kingdom of God is in the world in terms of its function. The world is the soil, the church is the sower. The world is a dark house, God's people a candle. The world is a field where the weeds, which are the wicked, and the wheat, which is the church, grow side by side. The church is the mustard seed that becomes a great tree. The world is the flour, the church the

leaven mixed in by God to make the dough rise. The world is the
sea containing fish of all kinds, the church is the net cast into it
by the angels. The world is the earth, the church its salt and light.
Thus, between the world as God's creation and the church there
is no discontinuity.[1]

The church needs the world. What good is a seed without soil
in which to grow, a net without a sea, or leaven without dough?
But the church's function is always clearly defined. It is not the
world; it does not perform the world's tasks nor is it responsible to
direct its affairs. The church is in the world, but not of it.

Seeking Divine Justice

If by "world" we mean the fallen order, then Jesus does not seem
to draw a clear-cut distinction between the world and the state.
The state exists in the realm of the relative. Even if its institutions
are the deposit left by religious traditions of the past, it should
never claim to be absolute or be given absolute status. It stands
under the judgment of God, as do all human activities.[2] And yet
God desires its conversion as he desires the conversion of every
individual.

The relationship between church and state can perhaps best be
grasped in the parable of the unrighteous judge:

> In a certain town there was a judge who neither feared God nor cared
> about men. And there was a widow in that town who kept coming
> to him with the plea, "Grant me justice against my adversary."
>
> For some time he refused. But finally he said to himself, "Even
> though I don't fear God or care about men, yet because this widow
> keeps bothering me, I will see that she gets justice, so that she
> won't eventually wear me out with her coming!"
>
> Listen to what the unjust judge says. And will not God bring
> about justice for his chosen ones, who cry out to him day and
> night? Will he keep putting them off? I tell you, he will see that
> they get justice, and quickly. However, when the Son of Man
> comes, will he find faith on the earth? (Luke 18:1–8)

This town is surely like one of the little cities in New Testament times. At the head of each municipality was a judge who applied the law and settled differences. This particular judge had neither fear of God nor respect for his fellows. The text says literally: "He would not turn back for man." How severely Jesus described the authorities of his time! The precision of his description suggests that he was alluding to the actual situation in Palestinian towns under occupation: shady tax-gatherers, brutal Roman centurions, corrupt judges with no regard for God's law.

Are things much better in our own time? The world is still divided between master-peoples, enjoying their full rights, and subject-peoples who are colonized and exploited. In times of war, at least, governments reveal their true character; the question of governing in the fear of God does not even arise. In wartime the Ten Commandments and the Golden Rule are altogether set aside.[3] What would become of us if our government "turned back" for a man dying on a battlefield, for a woman or a child trapped in a blazing fire?

It seems Jesus accepted as inevitable the injustice of the town's administration. The rich and powerful triumph, the poor, the widows, and the orphans are exploited. "What can I do about it?" the unjust judge tells himself. "It has always been like this; I have to pass judgment in concrete situations and can't escape into a utopian dream world." Jesus would have agreed. But he refused to be a judge of this kind (Luke 12:14). The church, then, should also not involve itself in state administration or the arbitration of human conflicts. It has another task.

Had it not been for the widow in this parable, all would have gone on as usual. But she was an obstacle. Perhaps the widow represents the church, as Jesus hinted when he identified her with "the chosen ones." (God chose a people for himself from among the nations: Israel. The new Israel, which is the church, is also chosen. But the church, unlike Israel of old, has no racial or geographical boundaries.)

The church is the widow, placed in the town to carry out her mission. She is poor, without influence and without rights, like the early Christians. She is the little flock described by the prophets as "the remnant of Israel." She is among the humble celebrated by Mary in her song (Luke 1:46–55). This is the true nature of the church.

But the poor widow is not resigned to her lot. To be sure, she is no revolutionary waiting to overthrow the judge's authority. She respects his authority even in its injustices, and she appeals to him to grant justice. But she will not give in and does not seek alms. She is oppressed, taken advantage of by her adversary, and seeks justice.

Here is the widow in intimate contact with the unjust state. Is she going to convert the judge, bring the state to repentance, have it confess its fault and fall at the feet of God? No. After a lengthy resistance the judge, thinking the case over, will make an exception. She pesters him, comes back again and again to drive him crazy. To get rid of her, he sees justice done. Does the judge give in merely because he is weary? Does not the worst tyrant feel some mysterious respect for the man or woman of courage?

The judge yields. He does not henceforth adopt the Sermon on the Mount as his norm, yet he gives in on one point. And so other plaintiffs, and the widow herself, will be able to invoke the precedent to obtain justice once again. In this way the church will fulfill its function in society. It will not itself govern, but it is the cornerstone of divine justice, and the state must either build on it or else stumble over it to its own condemnation.

Some readers will say this parable was intended merely to show us that we must "always pray and never lose heart." Indeed we must. But is the prayer that Jesus taught us, "Hallowed be your

JESUS AND THE NONVIOLENT REVOLUTION

name, your kingdom come, your will be done on earth as it is in heaven," simply an affair between God and the individual soul? Is it only concerning their own salvation that the elect cry day and night to God? Is it only for *their* forgiveness, for assurance of *their* redemption?

In this parable Jesus speaks of the need for a justice of a far broader kind. He is saying to the church: Pray, pray the prayer I have taught you, that is, claim from God the restoration of justice on the earth, a resounding victory over evil. The church is not just a little flock of souls saved from death and awaiting God's final judgment of the world. No, for Jesus the state – the unjust judge – is encircled. Its position is a precarious one between God, who holds it in his hand and judges it from on high, and the church, whose ceaseless prayer will be answered. For the judge will be obliged to yield, so persistent are the widow's pleas. Our prayer is a lever, its fulcrum God. Bearing down on it with all their weight in the name of divine justice, the believing ones move the mountain of injustice in the world.

The parable ends with a new twist. Yes, it is God who brings about his justice on earth, it is he who makes the claims. However, he will do nothing without his elect. He expects the church to have faith, that is, to intercede below as a forerunner of the divine justice that comes from on high. If justice is not done promptly, if the widow continues to be exploited, if the judge persists in his contempt for God and humanity, if the church remains unheard, then the fault lies in its lack of faith, the mediocrity of its protests, its lack of a true spirit of prayer, and its tendency to compromise with evil and the unjust authorities of the world.

What a strange conclusion. The church, if unfaithful, is no longer compared to the widow suffering injustice, but to the salt of the earth that has lost its savor and is, therefore, responsible for the corruption of the world.

Conscience versus Concession

What is a Christian to do, then, in countries where the state, without being Christian, has been sufficiently influenced by the church to guarantee fundamental rights? Must this state be abandoned into the hands of the unbelieving? In refusing to defend it, do not Christians risk hastening its decline and so find themselves a party to the ruin of the fragile edifice of freedom erected by the faithfulness of their fathers?

The answer to this is clear: it is our faithfulness to our calling as God's envoys that will insure the survival of the democratic state. On the other hand, service given blindly to a state will lead to its decay. Besides, the "freedoms" and privileges we would defend are a burden for the peoples we exploit without realizing it. The church must never give allegiance to the state, even if the state protects it, but must constantly call the state to a more perfect justice.

Jesus gave two metaphors that show the role of the church in a country that is well-disposed toward it: the lamp giving light to the house, and the eye as the lamp of the body. In the first metaphor, the church is the light of the world (Matt. 5:14–16); it must make its good deeds shine. In the second, the church is the eye, or the conscience, of the body (Luke 11:33–36). The lamp in the house lights all those who come in. The eye, the lamp of the body, lights up the whole body; no part of it remains in darkness.

Jesus himself spoke often of light and identified himself with it. He also explicitly told his disciples to be the light of the world.[4] It is impossible to regard this teaching about light as marginal. We can safely conclude that the parable of the eye as the light of the body defines quite naturally the function of the church in the world, which is to be the world's conscience.

So while the widow's mission is one of contradiction, the function of the lamp and of the eye is constructive. No one lights a candle to put it under a bowl. An eye is of no use in dark.

Yet today's church is fast becoming dim. Indeed, throughout history the church has allowed its visual faculty to be impaired and has allowed itself to be put under a bowl. Then darkness falls on the house, and the blind run into and injure one another. The body plunged into darkness stumbles and falls. So it is with the world. If the church ceases to exercise its illuminating function, the world falls into confusion.

The eye needs the other organs of the body. But we must not think that just because it is dependent on the world, the church must make concessions to it. It should never renounce the exercise of its particular function, which is to *see*. To do so would be nothing but betrayal.

One might well imagine a scene at the Last Judgment, before the throne of God. There, side by side in the dock, are the state and the church. God addresses the state first, demanding an account of its crimes: "Why did you tolerate the exploitation of the poor? Why have you oppressed, persecuted, tortured, and murdered? Why did you make war on other nations, devastating their cities and killing by the millions?" The state will bow its head, knowing it has sinned, and will ask for pardon. It will also plead an extenuating circumstance. "The church here," it will argue, "never translated your commandments into practical deeds. It never prophesied or showed the way. Instead it became rich. It became an institution where earthly concerns tempered its zeal. It collaborated with me and gave me its blessing. It was because of its blindness that I went astray. I accept your judgment, but also ask that the church be more severely condemned."[5]

Then God will turn to the church and say, "Why did you say nothing when you saw the rich in your midst exploiting the people? Why did you pretend not to know what the state was doing, how it was oppressing, imprisoning, and torturing? Why did your members take part in its wars? It was not your part to be the soldier's foot, the hand or the brain of the nuclear technician, the arm of the artilleryman or the pilot, but the clear-sighted eye, alert and ready to give the body of the state warning of the abyss toward which it was moving."

God will not relent. "You were my chosen one, but you have renounced your vocation. You were charged with a special mission, but you cast it aside. Like Jonah, it was your fault that the storm broke loose and the ship almost foundered. If Jonah had not repented, Nineveh would not have heard his message, would not have repented, and would have been destroyed. Now you have not followed Jonah on the path of repentance, and because of *you* I am obliged to condemn the state."

There is yet hope for the church. The little oil lamps of Jesus' time were not very bright. Still, the difference between the total darkness of an unlighted house, and the light shed by a single lamp is the difference between night and day. As Jesus said, "It gives light to everyone in the house." Here is good news for Christ's disciples! We need not worry about the effectiveness of our preaching or of our example of nonresistance and gentleness. Our voice, if we would but speak, our example, if we would but put love into practice, is not lost in the night.

But Jesus sounds a warning: "See to it, then, that the light within you is not darkness." Politics per se are not the church's business. The church is not to preoccupy itself with results. It has not even to practice "pacifism," that is, reject arms with the object of stopping war. No, God expects only one thing of it: that it walk in obedience to the gospel, refusing violence in whatever form because of that obedience, without concerning itself with the consequences, good or bad, that such refusal may involve. Such faith puts into practice the justice that marks the Jubilee, God's kingdom. The church's business is not to establish peace between the nations, but to bear witness to the love of God, to live in his peace and righteousness.

Such simplicity will light up the world and oblige the states to put their houses in order. This order will not bring universal peace. There will still be wars and rumors of wars. But what matter? In the past there have been astounding miracles of God's response to his people's suffering and faith. Let us take care not to render such miracles impossible through our lack of faith.

CHAPTER SIXTEEN

God's History

From its inception, the way of nonviolence that Jesus' disciples inherited from their master has posed various problems, not the least of which is the problem of the church's relationship to the state. Despite considerable changes in the notions of church and state throughout the centuries, some Christians still try to find normative definitions of the church and the state in the Bible. This endeavor is useless, because it begins with a wrong assumption. It wrongly refers to "the church" and "the state" as if there were only one church and only one state in the world.

To be strictly objective, one should refer to churches (separated everywhere into national churches and into numerous denominations) and to states (trying to keep interior order, but divided into hostile governments that wage war with each other). If we adopt this terminology, it is obvious that the rules of submission to Caesar as they are deduced from, for example, Romans 13 are inadequate for our day. An altogether different frame of reference must be found if we are to make progress on this matter.

Kingdom Algebra

Some suggest we should give up trying to find a social ethic in the Bible altogether. The problem, however, is in their approach. The Bible relates "slices of history" – the history of Israel among the nations, the history of Jesus among the Jews, the history of the apostles among the Gentiles. Each of these slices contains some revelation about the relationship between God and his people or between God's people and the world. The Bible attempts neither to define the nature of God nor the nature of society. Rather, it describes their relations and interactions.

When Jesus told his disciples, "You are the salt of the earth… you are the light of the world…you are the eye of the social body… you are my witnesses," he was not teaching them the "arithmetic" of the kingdom of God, that is, the technique of performing operations on absolute values. Rather, he was revealing the "algebra" of the kingdom of God, that is, the "functions and relations" between unknown values. Any speculation concerning the church and the state as absolute values is therefore unscriptural and doomed to failure.[1] Jesus viewed all man-made institutions as relative; they can be instruments of God, but only insofar as they are open to God's rulership.

The "algebraic formulas" found in the Bible still reveal God's will for his people. Though they do not give us the values of the unknowns, they allow us to explore and clear out large sections of the jungle of human society. Let us summarize a few of them.

First, Jesus' nonviolence finds its roots in the Jewish notion of a chosen people with a mission among the nations. Nonviolence is not a moral ideal but the fruition of God's plan of redemption in history *through a people.*[2] It is redemption that defines the people of God. And so even after many centuries, the church's defense against the enemies of truth still boils down to this: through Jesus Christ the church has inherited Israel's vocation as the Servant of the Lord. As such, the church can count on God alone for its defense.

Second, the chosen people must refuse to divorce justice and forgiveness. Justice and mercy follow each other in time, just as the Sabbath follows the six days of the week. The Sabbath foreshadows the final restoration of all things. Jesus wanted to restore the Sabbath and the Jubilee in Israel. Consequently, the awakening he started was revolutionary, from both a religious and a social standpoint. A great reversal was underway.[3] This is as needed in the world today as it was in Israel back then.

Third, Jesus did not have a pessimistic view of the world. He did not propose asceticism or withdrawal, or demand an "ethic of absolutes" impossible to practice in real life. Rather, he described behavior governed by the love of God and demonstrated its possibility in the world.

Fourth, Jesus' commitment to nonviolence did not grow out of a pantheistic, optimistic, or utopian view of the world. Instead, it came from a precise evaluation of the terrible power of evil. This became obvious in his act of redemption on the cross, through which God, and God alone, overcame the power of evil by using it for his glory. The church should continue to manifest this redemption.

Fifth, Jesus had a definite political program: the reestablishment of Israel by means of which the chosen people would become the light of the nations.[4] The body of Christ today is the new Israel, formed by those who have responded to Jesus' call of discipleship. The contemporary church has thus inherited Jesus' revolutionary program. It must therefore again and again repent and reform itself according to Jesus' sabbatical and jubilean vision, inaugurating the coming kingship of Christ over the world with concrete actions.

Sixth, Jesus never abandoned his original mission. His revolutionary nonviolence was not founded on the weakness of a God who gave up doing justice. Jesus announced the imminence of the judgment and the eschatological kingdom.[5] But because of the chosen people's disobedience, and because of the sacrifice of his Son, God has delayed his judgment and is now showing his love for the world by granting it an opportunity for repentance. This salvation, of which the church is both the beneficiary and the messenger, is meant for all individuals and all nations.

Seventh, and lastly, during this delay—inaugurated by Jesus' sacrifice—God always saves; he never kills. He places the individual person, whether good or evil, at the center of his history. Every person must be healed. By embracing the person, Jesus reveals that we are capable of understanding the person of God, our Father. The object of nonviolence, the fabric of which it is knit, is the individual person, always unique in the sight of God, since the unique Son of God sacrificed his life for this person.

Engaging History Faithfully

To my knowledge, all the religious, philosophical, and political doctrines that affirm the inevitable use of violence also acknowledge that it is secondary. Violence is only a means of reaching a desirable end: justice and peace. But peace is nonviolence. In this sense all agree that nonviolence is their final aim.[6]

Consequently, those who abandon nonviolence—the supreme goal of human endeavor—by participating in certain "necessary" violent actions in order to fulfill their human duty, are not exhibiting a genuine sense of history. In fact, they are bypassing history, freezing history, betraying history insofar as they abandon its supreme goal. Woe to humanity on the day when Christians give up being the salt of the earth and capitulate to the violent ones! Christ's followers are to draw history out of the mire by proving that nonviolent action, the visible expression of redemption, is the only means by which to bring about peace and justice.[7]

Unfortunately, the Christian faith is still plagued by the victory of Greek philosophy over Jesus' Jewish roots. The idea of establishing the kingdom of God sounds as foreign to our modern ears as it did to the Greek contemporaries of Jesus. It is no wonder that the early church's compromise with Plato shrank Christian hope for this world down to almost nothing. Spirit and matter were separated. Since the church thought of this earthly life as fleeting, over the centuries it tended to ignore or downplay political and social problems. The earth, it taught, is a "valley of tears" where God puts humankind through various trials, an arena of testing where God sorts out the good and the bad, the saved and the damned, the candidates for heaven and those for perdition.

Consequently, war, injustice, sickness, and poverty are no longer considered obstacles to the kingdom of God. Instead, they are trials God sends to his people before receiving them into heaven. We are to accept them without questioning God's mysterious intentions. Resignation is the prize virtue, a virtue for which every Christian is to strive during his or her journey on earth. By eliminating pride and the desires of the flesh, the believer can be assured of going straight to paradise.

In order to justify itself, the church has relegated Jesus' teaching to a separate sphere. Instead of the gospel, it emphasizes norms required of everyone, the natural order of things as created by God, and the virtue of performing the "duties of one's station."[8] The child, the adolescent, the husband, the wife, the citizen, the farmer, the factory worker, the employer, the employee, the politician, the police officer, the soldier, the diplomat—all will conscientiously perform the duties of their station. The world, although it is imperfect and sinful, is not completely abandoned by God. At every level of life, God has placed human authorities in charge of maintaining the order he has instituted. If everyone does his humble job, all will be well.

Yet if the history of Christianity, especially in Europe, has shown us anything, it is the fallacy of such ideas. After the fall of the Roman Empire and its schism into antagonistic countries, each prince believed he carried the sword in the name of God. This belief caused centuries of general anarchy, civil wars, crusades, persecutions against heretics, and religious wars. Each prince imposed on his subjects the religion of his choice. Had not Paul said, "He who rebels against the authority is rebelling against what God has instituted" (Rom. 13:2)?

In the eighteenth century many sought to instill tolerance into the chaos. But the visionaries of that day did not meet their expectations. To stop tyranny, the "tolerant" people used the guillotine. Since then, parliamentary and authoritarian regimes have succeeded each other, all in the name of Christian ideals. The church obeys the authorities "for conscience' sake," since Christian values are at the very least recognized and protected. However, the atrocities of two world wars between Christian peoples have shown the absurdity of such obedience.[9]

One of the positive outcomes of these atrocities has been the church's hesitation to teach, as it did in the past, that governing authorities come straight from God. But the church stops there. It does not dare to go back to the nonviolence of Jesus and the first Christians. "Since you are not sure about your duty," it tells its members, "be submissive to the authorities. It is the solution with the fewest risks."

So Christians today continue to submit themselves unthinkingly. The Christian is a good father, a good citizen, a good worker, a good soldier. No one mentions to him the imminence of God's kingdom with its religious, social, and political implications. Tormented consciences are provided with magnificent shelters of euphoric international conferences, subtle theological discussions, splendid liturgies, and the vague hopes mentioned in religious hymns.

We must be courageous enough to state flatly that the ethic of the "duties of station" or, as some would say, "callings," is nothing more than a contemporary rendition of Pharisaism. The church has substituted man-made tradition and reason for the kingdom and justice of God. Today's "Christian citizen kits" are very well equipped, whether they be Russian, German, French, or American. Like their Jewish ancestors, many of today's Christian citizens scrupulously tithe mint and dill and cummin, but neglect the weightier matters of the law—justice, mercy, and faithfulness. They, too, are "blind guides."

It is not at all surprising, then, that the church has lost its power to witness. True, the church supplies society with honest citizens who carry out their responsibilities. It comforts the poor, whom society neglects. It consoles the dying, for whom medical science has given up hope.[10] But for most Christians today faith amounts to little more than overcoming fear in the face of life's hardships. And sometimes it does not even go that far! At night, when modern man goes to bed, he no longer prays for his salvation, no longer awaits a kingdom of God, a kingdom he no longer needs, but instead grows impatient because science has not yet succeeded in landing someone on Mars.

Thy Kingdom Come

Of course, criticizing our current situation is not the answer. It is not the masses who have abandoned the church; rather the church has given up answering the questions people are asking: What will be the outcome of overpopulation: famine or war? What will happen to humanity if nuclear war breaks out? If a totalitarian regime takes over, what will be the future of my country, of my language, of my civilization, and of the moral values they represent? What is the goal of modern science? Will technology free the world from hunger and ignorance or will it enslave us to the computer? What can I do with my limited material and

intellectual resources and my dependence on society for my livelihood? How can I provide for the future of my children, improve
society, prevent war, or contribute to the establishment of justice
and peace?

To each of these questions the church gives nothing but vague
and wordy answers. Yet all one needs to do is read the Gospels to
see that the problems facing a Jew of the first century were similar
to those facing us today. "What will happen to humanity," this
Jew was wondering, "if Rome crushes all these nations under its
material power? What will happen to my people if the worship of
the emperor destroys faith in the true God? What will happen if
Israel's divine calling becomes the laughingstock of the wise men
of our day? Will Greek culture bring an era of universal peace or
will it plunge the world into chaotic immorality? What can I as a
Jew, limited by my human resources and my dependence on the
society that gives me my daily bread, do to become an instrument
of God and prepare the way for the coming of the Messiah?"

To these questions of his contemporaries, Jesus gave a concrete
answer: "The kingdom of God is near. Repent and believe the
good news!" (Mark 1:15). He proclaimed the jubilean revolution
and the restoration of Israel by arousing the enthusiasm of the
oppressed and the faith of the poor. Something brand-new was
about to happen if people would but accept it.

In Jesus' time, Jews could feel the end of the Jewish state
approaching, identified it with the end of the world, and thought
in apocalyptic terms. Similarly, today we can vaguely feel that the
end of Western civilization is near, though it is still at the height
of its splendor. Belief in the imminent coming of God's kingdom
once again becomes real. Rationalistic philosophies of the past are
losing their brilliance in the distance. The shelters of tradition-
alism, liturgy, and mysticism are beginning to look like escape
mechanisms. Youth thirsts for action. Action for what purpose? It

does not know. But one must go faster, higher, farther; one must produce more or destroy more, no matter what the cost. Destroy what? Unjust structures? No one knows exactly how.

In such a context one should wonder whether the coming kingdom is not about to become a reality, here and now.

"It is a myth!" say the intellectuals. But history is moved by myths.[11] There is the myth of laissez-faire in the eighteenth century, the myths of the triumph of science and perpetual progress in the nineteenth century, the myths of the inescapable advent of socialism and of the master race in the twentieth century.

Over and against these senseless modern myths invented by humans to justify their superiority complexes, which put the human race in competition with the Creator himself, there is the "myth" of the God of goodness, who has chosen people to prepare a kingdom of justice, truth, and love on earth. This myth dies hard. It always comes back throughout history in different forms, especially following massacres where we have outdone ourselves in criminality. Are not the League of Nations of the past, the Socialist International, and the United Nations reflections—very dim, of course, but nonetheless very moving ones—of humanity's hope for God's kingdom?

Truly the expectation of the kingdom of God is the mysterious guide of history. Economic factors and technological discoveries are merely used by human hope to build a better future. Why then should we refuse to recognize the revealed origin of this hope for the kingdom of God? Why should we refuse to admit that Christ taught it to us? When one must choose between nothingness and the kingdom, how can one choose anything but the kingdom?

Perhaps to end our study it will be helpful to draw an analogy. With only one eye we perceive all objects in the same plane. This can easily be verified by closing one eye; you lose your sense of depth. But nature gave us two eyes, and the distance between them enables each eye to perceive objects from a slightly different angle. If you close and open each eye alternately, you will soon become aware of this fact. To focus on an object near us, we have to cross our eyes slightly to avoid a double image. If, on the other hand, you look at an object in the distance, the objects in the foreground will form double images. Our brain corrects this double image on our retinas by "forgetting" the splitting of the foreground objects, which become annoying when we are conscious of them.

One eye by itself has no sense of depth. The effort of the ocular muscles allows the brain to reconstitute the depth of different objects. The nervous system can then coordinate the effort of the eyes with the efforts of the motor muscles. A newborn child has no sense of depth, but he has two eyes. As soon as he can grasp objects and walk, he learns to see "correctly" and move among the obstacles around him without bumping into them.

Let us now apply this to our discussion. Let us assume that we have two eyes, two visions of the world, an exterior vision that enables us to perceive the sensible world, reality "as it is," and an interior vision, which reveals to us the kingdom, reality "as it should and will be."

We are like a child who cannot yet superimpose the two images. Each image is flat. Indeed, the world "as it is" has no depth; it is a sequence of phenomena with no rhyme or reason, without origin or end. Similarly the world "as it should and will be," the kingdom, is flat. Isolated from the sensible world, it remains an ideal without substance, because ideas need the support of matter to become realities.

As adults, we should be capable of seeing reality with stereoscopic vision. Our eyes and our spirit should be able to superimpose these two images of the world. Each of these images would at the same time gain relief, depth, and meaning that mon-ocular vision cannot give.

Jesus Christ is the adult whose vision has completely superim-posed the world as it is and the kingdom of God, thus gaining a depth of vision into the nature of things, and into the origin and the end of humanity. How can we ever find a correct vision of the world? A sure place to stand? Only if we make the "muscular" effort necessary to gain a stereoscopic vision of the world as Jesus saw it: "Behold, the kingdom of God is at hand."

To see the world correctly in relief and depth is to act by faith in obedience to Jesus. Whenever people submit themselves to Christ, the superposition of these two images of the world incites a revolution. Such people live and act in the world in the pure light of the coming kingdom of God.

Notes

Square brackets indicate notes added by the editor of this edition.

Introduction

1. [For the best account of what happened in Le Chambon sur Lignon see Pierre Sauvage's documentary, *Weapons of the Spirit*. Additional information can be found in the following: Stuart A. Kallen, *The Faces of Resistance* (Minneapolis: Abdo Consulting Group, 1944); Susan Zucotti, *The Holocaust, the French and the Jews* (New York: Harper Collins, 1993); Eva Fogelman, *Conscience and Courage* (New York: Anchor Books, 1994); F. Rochat and André Modiglian, "The Ordinary Quality of Resistance" in *Journal of Social Issues* 51, no. 3 (1995), pp. 195–210. Philip Hallie's influential book, *Lest Innocent Blood Be Shed,* though inspiring and informative, is neither historically nor biographically accurate. It tends to sensationalize and romanticize Trocmé's role in the rescue efforts. Nevertheless, it was the first book to put the story of Le Chambon on the map. *Lest Innocent Blood Be Shed: The Story of Le Chambon and How Goodness Happened There* (New York: Harper & Row, 1979). Trocmé's personal memoir is now available to the public at Swarthmore College. It has yet to be translated into English.]

2. [Trocmé's and Theis's sermon of June 23, 1940, from the Magda and André Trocmé Papers, Swarthmore College Library, Peace Collection.]

3. [2,500 is Trocmé's own estimate. Some place the number as high as 5,000.]

4. [Unlike the social gospel movement at the turn of the twentieth century, or some liberation theologies that have emerged since, Trocmé resists abstracting a set of norms from the gospel that ends up merely reflecting one's own political mindset. He seriously engages the biblical text in the context of its time.]

Preface

[1] [Trocmé is referring here to the work of Ernst Käsemann and the "new quest" that followed in the late 1950s. Trocmé could not have known of a "third quest" that began in the early 1980s and continues with great fervor. For a helpful survey of the various quests for Jesus, see Craig L. Blomberg, *Jesus and the Gospels* (Nashville: Broadman & Holman, 1997), pp. 179–187, and Ben Witherington, III, *The Jesus Quest: The Third Search for the Jew of Nazareth* (Downers Grove, Ill.: InterVarsity, 1995).]

[2] [The majority of current New Testament scholars concur with Trocmé on this point. See E. P. Sanders, *Jesus and Judaism* (Philadelphia: Fortress, 1985); N.T. Wright, *Jesus and the Victory of God* (Minneapolis: Fortress, 1996); and John P. Meier, *A Marginal Jew: Rethinking the Historical Jesus*, 3 vols. (New York: Doubleday, 1991–1994; New York: Anchor, 2001).]

[3] On the subject of the biblical Jubilee, I had recourse to an article by F. M. Lemoine, O.P., "Le jubilé dans la Bible," *Vie Spirituelle* 81, no. 345 (Oct. 1949), as well as to the exhaustive work by Robert North, S.J., *Sociology of the Biblical Jubilee*, Analecta Biblica, no. 4 (Rome: Pontifical Biblical Institute, 1954).

Chapter 1: Jesus the Jew

[1] [Much is now known about the syncretistic world of the Gospels. For an extensive treatment of the various groups and movements in Palestine, see Ekkehard W. Stegemann and Wolfgang Stegemann, *The Jesus Movement: A Social History of Its First Century* (Minneapolis: Fortress, 1999), ch. 6.]

[2] The Gospels of Matthew, Mark, and Luke.

[3] See Matt. 14:5; 21:23–26, 46.

[4] [N. T. Wright confirms Trocmé's thesis: "Jesus' critique of his contemporaries was a critique from within; his summons was not to abandon Judaism and try something else but to become the true, returned-from-exile people of the one true God. His aim was to be the means of God's reconstitution of Israel." N. T. Wright, *The Challenge of Jesus: Rediscovering Who Jesus Was and Is* (Downers Grove, Ill.: InterVarsity, 1999), p. 52. George Pixley concludes similarly: "Jesus and his movement did not see Rome as the principal enemy. In their priorities, it was first necessary to do away with the temple domination…Jesus and his followers had tried to unite the people against the temple because they believed that *it* rather than the Romans was the primary source of Israel's oppression." George V. Pixley, *God's Kingdom: A Guide for Biblical Study* (Maryknoll, N.Y.: Orbis, 1981), pp. 80–82.]

⁵ [Although Trocmé is referring to communist and socialist movements in Europe, and not to current Third World "liberation theologies," these later movements, with their base communities, confirm his point.]

⁶ [The themes of election, disobedience, and restoration run throughout the Old Testament. See especially Isa. 19:19ff., 25:6–8, 49:8ff., 56:1ff., and Jer. 29:10–14, 31:23ff., 33:6–9.]

⁷ Cf. Matt. 21:42–44, 23:1ff.; Luke 13:22–35.

⁸ In the history of Christianity, the notion of a paradise after death has often replaced the eschatological notion of the kingdom of God.

⁹ Gen. 3:17–19, 6:5–7. Some argue that the story of Creation and the Fall comes from a Sumerian myth. Even so, it was the Jews with their particular outlook who derived a thoroughly ethical story from the legend.

¹⁰ The "offense" that God's Word inflicts on us is the only starting point of a life renewed by God's grace.

¹¹ Despite the relative leniency of modern law, our society still resorts to "blood vengeance" in its most inhuman form. It assumes the right to inflict appalling collective punishments on entire nations. The soldier is the modern "avenger of blood." While carrying out his sacred task, he stains his hands with the blood of others, yet supposedly remains innocent in God's eyes, whose works he executes.

¹² [The *lex talionis* was essentially a requirement of restraint meant to reduce the level of violence. Its thrust was: "No more than a life for a life, no more than an eye for an eye…" See Gardner C. Hanks, *Against the Death Penalty: Christian and Secular Arguments Against Capital Punishment* (Scottdale, Pa.: Herald Press, 1997), chs. 1 & 2.]

Chapter 2: Jesus Proclaims Jubilee

¹ The words in parentheses are found in Luke's text, but not in Isaiah 61, quoted by Jesus.

² [For a discussion on dating this text, see William W. Klein, "The Sermon at Nazareth (Luke 4:14–22)" in *Christian Freedom: Essays in Honor of Vernon C. Grounds,* ed. K. W. M. Wozniak and S. J. Grenz (Lanham, Md.: University Press of America, 1986).]

³ [Elsewhere the Gospels indicate that Jesus persistently avoided claiming he was the Messiah (John 10:24). Yet in quoting Isaiah 61 at the beginning of his ministry, Jesus unambiguously declared himself the Messiah, and implied that all his subsequent miracles of healing were proof of his messiahship (cf.

Luke 7:18–23). The matter is hermenuetically complex. For more on the "deep irony here," see Richard B. Hays, *The Moral Vision of the New Testament: A Contemporary Introduction to New Testament Ethics,* (New York: Harper San Francisco, 1996), pp. 116, 132.]

4 [Isaiah apparently meant "poor" literally. Jeremias points out, however, that "poor" includes both material and spiritual want. J. Jeremias, *New Testament Theology* (New York: Charles Scribner's Sons, 1971), p. 113.]

5 [Jesus' listeners may also have turned on him because, by mentioning the widow of Zarephath and Naaman of Syria, he suggested that the good news to the poor is also good news to Gentiles. See chapter 11 as well as Richard H. Lowery, *Sabbath and Jubilee* (St. Louis, Mo.: Chalice Press, 2000), p. 138; and G. R. Beasley-Murray, *Jesus and the Kingdom of God* (Grand Rapids, Mich.: Eerdmans, 1986), p. 90.]

6 To better understand the following discussion, the reader should consult the Old Testament texts which institute the sabbatical year: Leviticus 25 (which describes the Jubilee in detail); Exodus 21:2–6, 23:10–12; Deuteronomy 15:1–18, 31:9–13; Ezekiel 46:16–18; Jeremiah 34:8–17; Leviticus 26:34–38, 43; 2 Chronicles 36:20–21. [Luke 4:16–21 is by far the clearest reference in the Gospels to any of the Jubilee texts. This is not to suggest that the Nazareth speech alone is enough to prove that Jesus meant to inaugurate a Jubilee. See Sharon Ringe, *Jesus, Liberation, and Biblical Jubilee* (Philadelphia: Fortress, 1985), p. 44.]

7 ["When Jesus proceeded to affirm, 'Today the scripture has been fulfilled in your hearing,' they would have understood him to be announcing that the Jubilee had arrived, that the acceptable year of the Lord had begun…The statement is not simply a scripture quotation, therefore; it is a declaration that the time has arrived…Moreover, the Spirit of the Lord has anointed him to make known this good news and to put it into effect…The *proclamation* of release is accompanied by *acts* of release, as elsewhere in the preaching of Jesus." G. R. Beasley-Murray, *Jesus and the Kingdom of God,* pp. 88–89.]

8 The French version to which the author is referring translates Isaiah as "pay the debt of their iniquity" (translator's note).

9 Cf. Isa. 49:8; 58:5; Ps. 119:108.

10 Was Jesus intentionally emphasizing God's redemption over his vengeance? Cf. the section concerning the *goel* at the end of chapter 1.

11 [The idea of liberating slaves was not unique to Israel. In Egypt, for example, "release" was often granted to convicts, rebels, and to those exiled from home. John Dominic Crossan, *The Birth of Christianity* (New York: Harper San Francisco, 1998), p. 195.]

¹² [The basic idea of *shemittah* "is that the one who holds the loan must 'loosen his grip' (literally, 'release his hand') on the debtor's obligation to repay. He must 'drop it.' The law of release, *shemittah,* then, is the exact opposite of being tightfisted toward needy neighbors. It is a concrete gesture of opening the hand to the poor." Richard H. Lowery, *Sabbath and Jubilee,* p. 41.]

¹³ Luke's Greek source, the Old Testament Septuagint, translates both the *shemittah* of Deuteronomy and the *derôr* of Isaiah and Leviticus as *aphesis.*

¹⁴ When Jesus presented himself to John the Baptist to be baptized, he overcame John's hesitation by saying, "Let it be so now (*aphes arti,* literally "release at this time"); it is proper for us to do this to fulfill all righteousness" (Matt. 3:15). Matthew then says that John the Baptist consented (*aphiesin auton,* literally "released him"). Could these words indicate that Jesus wanted his baptism to have some jubilean significance? Before proclaiming liberty to the captives, did Jesus choose to inaugurate the Jubilee for himself with this act, establishing baptism as the first act of this liberation? This will require further inquiry.

¹⁵ [The same language is used in both versions of the Lord's Prayer (Matt. 6:9–15; Luke 11:2–4). See chapter 3 for further comments.]

¹⁶ See Mark 3:5; 8:25; etc. ["To us healing would seem distinct from the more political acts of liberating prisoners and ending oppression. But to the Hebrews, physical healing and economic or political deliverance did not belong to separate spheres. Their juxtaposition in Isaiah 61:1 is not unique. In Psalm 146, for example, the opening of the eyes of the blind is parallel to such divine actions as executing justice for the oppressed, setting prisoners free, and upholding the widow and fatherless (vv. 7–9). Thus it is appropriate for Matthew to view Jesus' acts of healing as the fulfillment of the prediction that the Servant of the Lord would establish justice (Matt. 12:18–21; Isa. 42:1–4). Malachi had promised that the sun of justice would 'rise with healing in his wings' (Mal. 4:2)." Stephen Charles Mott, *Biblical Ethics and Social Change* (New York: Oxford University Press, 1982), pp. 92–93.]

¹⁷ Some maintain the Jubilee was held every fifty years. This is an open debate.

¹⁸ See Ezek. 45:7–8, 46:16–18.

¹⁹ This idea of "investment" is found in certain parables of Jesus (Matt. 25:14–30; Luke 20:9–16). In conformity with the jubilean principle this investment is limited in time. Once the time has passed, the capital must be returned to God, the sole owner.

²⁰ [Whether the Jubilee was ever practiced and how it functioned are questions of extensive debate. Although it cannot be proven that such legislation was ever standard practice, there are plenty of examples that it was promulgated at

various times. See Robert Gnuse, *You Shall Not Steal: Community and Property in the Biblical Tradition* (Maryknoll, N.Y.: Orbis, 1985), ch. 3. Crossan notes that "The Jubilee Year may be a utopian ideal, but it is so formulated as to be actually possible." He quotes Josephus, who gives three examples of how to implement it not mentioned in the Bible. John Dominic Crossan, *The Birth of Christianity*, p. 197.]

²¹ Nehemiah 5:1–13 not only recounts the stirring celebration of the Jubilee, it also describes the process by which the poor of Israel were forced to pawn their fields, vineyards, and houses in order to receive wheat or pay their taxes during a period of famine, and how they were forced to turn their children into slaves when they could not meet the demands of their creditors. Jesus describes this same process in his parable of the unforgiving servant (Matt. 18:21ff.).

²² Flavius Josephus, *Jewish Antiquities*, XII, IX, 5. However, Josephus dates the sabbatical year as 164–163 B.C. This does not contradict the First Book of the Maccabees. Until the harvest following the sabbatical year, people relied upon the harvest of the preceding year. Consequently, 163–162 B.C. would have been the year the population felt the pinch of hunger.

²³ Ibid., XIII, VIII, 1 and XIV, XVI, 2. If one uses the first dates given by Josephus as points of reference, the sabbatical year should have occurred in 40–39 B.C., not 38–37 B.C. Remember that Josephus was writing 100 to 250 years after the events he reported, at a time when there were no newspapers.

²⁴ Setting the beginning of Jesus' ministry at such an early date creates difficulties, especially with Luke's chronology. Luke, with his great concern for accuracy, sets the beginning of John the Baptist's ministry in the fifteenth year of Emperor Tiberius' reign (Luke 3:1–2). Because Tiberius came into power in A.D. 19, John the Baptist's ministry would have started in A.D. 28. But many authoritative exegetes estimate that Jesus died before Passover of A.D. 28, and Jesus could hardly have been crucified before the beginning of John the Baptist's ministry! Historians have managed to resolve the difficulty. As early as A.D. 11, Tiberius was associated with the power of the weakening Emperor Augustus. It is possible that Luke counted fifteen years from that date, which would add up to A.D. 26.

Such a chronology coincides with a detail found in the Gospel of John. He places the expulsion of the merchants from the temple at the beginning of Jesus' ministry, shortly after the celebration of the Passover. On this occasion, the Jews tell Jesus, "It has taken forty-six years to build this temple, and will you raise it up in three days?" Herod the Great began construction of the temple in 20 B.C., so the words recorded in John 2:20, which date the beginning of Jesus' ministry in Jerusalem, would have been uttered in the spring of A.D. 27.

This brief study of dates seems to confirm our thesis. When John the

Baptist began his "cry in the desert" in A.D. 26, Jesus was among the first to be baptized. Soon after the temptation, he would have returned to Galilee where he began preaching. In September A.D. 26 he proclaimed the Jubilee in Nazareth. During the Passover of A.D. 27, he went to Jerusalem. In A.D. 28, a year and a half after beginning his ministry, he was crucified in Jerusalem during the Passover.

Chapter 3: Implications of Jubilee

¹ [Yoder, in *The Politics of Jesus,* devotes an entire chapter to "The Implications of the Jubilee," in which he freely adapts Trocmé's work. Like Trocmé, Yoder traces the four prescriptions of the Jubilee in Luke's Gospel, noting that the jubilean vision underlies many of Jesus' teachings. He then reviews some of the critical scholarship on the Jubilee since the initial publication of his book in 1972, which concurs that jubilean themes run throughout the synoptic Gospels. At least for Luke, the Jubilee was a "platform statement" that characterized Jesus' public ministry. John Howard Yoder, *The Politics of Jesus,* 2nd ed. (Grand Rapids, Mich.: Eerdmans, 1994), ch. 3. At the very least, modern commentators recognize the programmatic thrust of the Nazareth speech. See John Nolland, *Luke 1–9:20,* Word Biblical Commentary (Waco, Tex.: Word, 1989), p. 195. Chilton even asserts that the sermon at Nazareth is a paradigm for Christian mission, both in terms of content and response. See B. Chilton, "Announcement in Nazareth: An Analysis of Luke 4:16–21," *Gospel Perspectives,* vol. 2, ed. R. J. France and D. Wenham (Sheffield, England: JSOT Press, 1981), p. 168.]

² [The Aramaic term for "debt" can also mean "sin," but literally in the Greek it denotes "money debt." In a broader sense it means "obligation." Geoffrey W. Bromily, ed., *Theological Dictionary of the New Testament: Abridged in One Volume* (Grand Rapids, Mich.: Eerdmans, 1985), p. 747.]

³ [For more on this, see Richard H. Lowery, *Sabbath and Jubilee,* pp. 139–140. Lowery also notes the jubilean features of the parable of the rich young man, pp. 140–142.]

⁴ The very existence of the *prosbul* shows that there was in Israel at the time of Jesus a strong current of opinion in favor of a strict application of the Jubilee's second provision, that is, the periodic remittance of debts. [For more on the *prosbul,* see Richard J. Cassidy, *Jesus, Politics, and Society: A Study of Luke's Gospel* (Maryknoll, N.Y.: Orbis, 1978), pp. 101–104.]

⁵ [Borg argues convincingly that Jesus' entire platform was one of compassion, in radical opposition to the Pharisees' agenda of ritual holiness. See Marcus J. Borg, *Conflict, Holiness, and Politics in the Teachings of Jesus* (Harrisburg, Pa.: Trinity Press International, 1998).]

⁶ Cf. Exod. 22:26.

⁷ Paul articulates a similar rationale in 1 Corinthians 6:1–8.

⁸ The exploitation of workers is less visible in the West than it was fifty years ago, but has expanded on an international scale. The hyper-industrialized countries draw their prosperity from the resources of underdeveloped regions. Multinational corporations that invest their capital in underdeveloped regions drain off dividends for their stockholders when the profits should be going to the inhabitants of these regions. A periodic redistribution of capital would avoid the bloody revolutions these cruel injustices inevitably cause. [Trocmé's argument is even truer today. See Walden Bello, *Dark Valley: The United States and Global Poverty,* new ed. (London: Pluto Press, 1999); and John Gray, *False Dawn: The Delusions of Global Capitalism* (New York: The New Press, 1998).]

⁹ [Commenting on Jesus' response to the rich young man (Mark 10:20 ff.), Myers argues that "the Jubilee ideology is the only plausible background to the conviction of Mark's Jesus that wealth must be redistributed as a precondition of the kingdom of God." Ched Myers, *Who Will Roll Away the Stone? Discipleship Queries for First World Christians* (Maryknoll, N.Y.: Orbis, 1995), p. 166.]

¹⁰ Exodus 22 also has a jubilean connotation. It orders "restitution" of alienated property. The Hebrew verb meaning "to restore" is *shalam* from which the substantive *shalom* (peace) derives. According to Moses, there is no peace without restitution or without justice.

¹¹ [At the very least, Jesus underscores the revolutionary socio-economic dimensions of the kingdom of God. "Yahweh's great Jubilee Year demanded a radical restructuring of all present social structures on the basis of the Covenant... All the actions of Jesus point in this same direction: his constant concern for bringing the outcast and the marginalized back into the community; his demand for love of neighbor and enemy...Furthermore, he demanded from those who would follow him equality by selling all they had and abandoning their social position...If one can agree that Jesus envisioned the kingdom in the setting of the restoration of Israel, then the Jubilee tradition was the best context for his message that he could have chosen. He saw the coming of God's reign in terms of a new people of God and of a new social order in this world." John Fuellenbach, *The Kingdom of God: The Message of Jesus Today* (Maryknoll, N.Y.: Orbis, 1995), pp. 128–129.]

Chapter 4: The "Politics" of Jesus

¹ [Hans Conzelmann's landmark, *The Theology of St. Luke* (New York: Harper & Row, 1960), argues essentially that Luke's Gospel was a "political apologetic."

According to Conzelmann, Jesus was not in conflict with the existing political order. His followers should therefore seek to act in harmony with the government. This view has been called into serious question. Cassidy points out that Jesus possessed a distinct "social stance." "Jesus offered a response, through his teachings and conduct, to the question of how persons and groups should live together...He responded not only to the social situation of the poor, the infirm, and the oppressed, but also to the policies and practices of the political leaders of his time." Cassidy, *Jesus, Politics, and Society,* p. 20. See also Borg, *Conflict, Holiness, and Politics in the Teachings of Jesus* and Yoder, *The Politics of Jesus,* ch. 4.

Even the term "gospel" *(euangélion)* has political import. In Greek it meant good news, especially news of victory in battle, or any imperial proclamation. When Jesus came preaching the gospel of the kingdom (Mark 1:14–15; Matt. 4:23; 9:35), it was good news of a royal, political nature.]

² [More accurately, there existed two primary social classes: urban and rural. The urban ruling elites (1–2%) and the service class (5–8%) exploited the rest, who were rural peasants. Stegemann and Stegemann, *The Jesus Movement,* chs. 4–5.]

³ However, when certain freedom fighters wanted to carry Jesus off to make him king (probably as a war leader) or when the people tried to make him a judge, he objected (John 6:14–15; Luke 12:14). We will later examine the reasons for this refusal.

⁴ The Gospels use the word *kerygma,* which means specifically the proclamation of a message by the king's heralds, a term with clear political connotations. See e.g. Matt. 10:27; Luke 9:2–6.

⁵ [Regarding the "political character" of Jesus' mission, Steidl-Meier makes the following important distinction: "It is important to distinguish between politics as struggle over legitimate authority and politics as a precise social agenda. I think that in the former sense Jesus was decidedly political, whereas in the latter he was only partially so...Thus the gospel does not present a precise program for all ages but suggests criteria by which any precise program may be evaluated." Paul Steidl-Meier, *Social Justice Ministry: Foundation and Concerns* (New York: Le Jacq Publishing, 1984), pp. 14–18.]

⁶ These remarks lead us to the distinction between the eschatological and the apocalyptic in Jesus' thought. Eschatology, knowledge of the "last things," is strongly rooted in history. It cannot be separated from the concrete history of the Jewish people or of the new Israel, the church. The hardships announced by the prophets are temporal ones, to be followed by the reestablishment of Israel on earth, where justice will reign from then on.

Apocalyptic thought, on the other hand, originates from the expectancy of a total destruction, which will affect not only the earth, but also the universe and will be followed by a new creation. The mingling of these two concepts is evident in Matthew 24.

7 [Crucifixion was standard punishment for political insurrection.]

8 [For further discussion on the meaning of the "Son of Man," see Marinus de Jonge, *Christology in Context: The Earliest Christian Response to Jesus* (Philadelphia: Westminster Press, 1988), pp. 169–172; and I. Howard Marshall, "Son of Man" in *Dictionary of Jesus and the Gospels,* eds. Joel B. Green and Scot McKnight (Downers Grove, Ill.: InterVarsity, 1992), pp. 775–781.]

9 Some exegetes claim that this was an evasive answer. (The Greek *su legeis* can be literally translated as "You have said so" (cf. Matt. 26:47–68; 27:11). But if Jesus tried to reassure Pilate with an evasive answer, why then did Pilate order the inscription "King of the Jews" to be put on the cross as the reason for Jesus' condemnation (Matt. 27:37; John 19:19–22)? Pilate would have been glad for an excuse to spare his life.

10 [Regarding Jesus' actions in and teachings on the temple, see Mark 11:15–17, 14:58, 15:29; John 2:13–19; Luke 13:34–35, 19:42–44, 21:20–24. For an extended treatment, see Borg, *Conflict, Holiness, and Politics in the Teachings of Jesus,* ch. 7.]

11 [Jesus' adversaries correctly understood him to be a political threat. Wright sums up the situation: "His attitude to the temple was not 'this institution needs reforming,' nor 'the wrong people are running this place,' nor yet 'piety can function elsewhere too.' His deepest belief regarding the temple was eschatological: the time had come for God to judge the entire institution. The temple had come to symbolize the injustice that characterized the society on the inside and the outside, the rejection of the vocation to be the light of the world, the city set on a hill that would draw to itself all the peoples of the world...

"[Jesus] believed that Israel's God was in the process of judging and redeeming his people, not just as one such incident among many but as the climax of Israel's history. This judgment would take the form of destruction by Rome. It would not...be followed by the rebuilding of a new physical temple. It would be followed by the establishment of the messianic community focused on Jesus himself that would replace the temple once for all." Wright, *The Challenge of Jesus,* pp. 52, 65–67. See also Cassidy, *Jesus, Politics, and Society,* p. 79.]

12 Most probably the empires of the Babylonians, the Medes, the Persians, and the Greeks. Jesus would probably have added the Roman Empire or the kingdom of the Herodian dynasty to the list.

[13] [Jesus' statement is a claim that he is ultimately not just the earthly Messiah, but the cosmic ruler who would come in glory and reign forever. F. F. Bruce, *The Hard Sayings of Jesus* (Downers Grove, Ill.: InterVarsity, 1983), pp. 245–247.

[14] The rest of this passage from Luke underlines the double nature of the kingdom, "…so that you may eat and drink at my table in my kingdom and sit on thrones judging the twelve tribes of Israel." This clearly evokes the banquet that will take place when the kingdom of God finally comes (Luke 22:18), and it is unclear whether it will be on earth or in heaven. [Current scholarly consensus sees the kingdom of God in Jesus' teachings as dual in nature: both present and future, eschatological and apocalyptic, temporal and eternal, social and spiritual. See e.g. Beasley-Murray, *Jesus and the Kingdom of God;* and Wendell Wills, ed., *The Kingdom of God in 20th Century Interpretation* (Peabody, Mass.: Hendrickson, 1987).]

[15] [See Craig S. Keener, *The IVP Bible Background Commentary: New Testament* (Downers Grove, Ill.: InterVarsity, 1993), pp. 241–242.]

Chapter 5: Ethics of the Revolution

[1] [It can be argued that Jesus deliberately chose the Sabbath as an issue over which to do battle. For Jesus, the Sabbath was an especially appropriate day for both the holiness and compassion of God to be active. Borg, *Conflict, Holiness, and Politics in the Teachings of Jesus,* ch. 6.]

[2] [Jesus makes the same point in his parable of the sheep and the goats (Matt. 25:31–46).]

[3] [Recall Jesus' rebuke of his contemporaries for turning the temple, a house of prayer, into a den of robbers.]

[4] [See e.g. C. H. Dodd, *The Apostolic Preaching and Its Developments* (Chicago: Willett, Clark & Co., 1937). The argument that the early church ethic of sharing was short-lived is problematic for two reasons: (1) The Jerusalem church was not unique in its attitude toward community of goods (2 Thess. 3:10; Eph. 4:28; 2 Cor. 8:13–15). In Rome alone, by A.D. 250 the relatively small Christian community was supporting 1500 people. See Eusebius, *Ecclesiastical History,* trans. J. E. L. Oulton (London: Heinemann, 1973), VI:43. (2) Throughout the history of the church there arose groups of Christians who, to a greater or lesser degree, "rediscovered" community of goods. See Trevor J. Saxby, *Pilgrims of a Common Life: Christian Community of Goods Through the Centuries* (Scottdale, Pa.: Herald Press, 1987).]

[5] [See Reinhold Niebuhr, *Interpretation of Christian Ethics* (New York: Harper, 1935).] "Situation ethics" would also fit this interpretation. The believer, faced

Notes

with the requirements of the kingdom of God, his own incapacity to do good, and the power of divine grace, receives in every situation the inspiration of the Holy Spirit and "invents" each time an answer that corresponds to God's direction.

6 [For further criticism of views that qualify or discount the ethical relevance of the Sermon on the Mount, see Hays, *The Moral Vision of the New Testament,* pp. 319–327.]

7 Jesus' ethic is adaptable because, though its goal is the kingdom of God, the delay God grants is not an empty one with vain tensions and endless conflicts, but a history, with Jubilees for landmarks, the first of which was inaugurated by Jesus. In every historical situation between Mount Sinai and the kingdom, the Spirit tells the church what form of injustice, violence, or false witness must be eliminated and in what terms the Jubilee must be proclaimed (e.g. James 2:1–13, 5:1–6). In this sense, Jesus' ethic is "situational," but not individually construed. It is an ethic of the church, no longer of leaderless snipers; a social ethic, no longer a sectarian one; a revolutionary ethic, no longer a static one; a concrete, practical ethic, no longer the hopeless struggle of a limping Israel with the angel of the absolute.

8 [It can be argued that Luke considered the communitarian practices of the early church to be paradigmatic. He emphasizes that *all* who believed had *everything* in common, and notes that they earned "the favor of all the people" (Acts 2:44–47). Clearly, the early church's economic sharing is "the first fruits of the mission that Jesus announced in Luke 4:16–21: to bring into being a restored Israel in which the good news is proclaimed and enacted for the poor and oppressed." Hays, *The Moral Vision of the New Testament,* p. 124. See also Stephen Charles Mott, *Biblical Ethics and Social Change,* p. 97.]

9 [Ched Myers convincingly argues that the apostle Paul understood the Jubilee as central to Christ's life and mission. Relying on the recent work of biblical scholars such as Elsa Tamez *(Amnesty of Grace),* Neil Elliott *(Liberating Paul),* and Richard Horsely *(Paul and Empire),* he argues that Paul, in jubilean fashion, was essentially egalitarian, subversive of imperial religion and politics, and an advocate for the poor. Ched Myers, "Balancing Abundance and Need," *The Other Side* 34, no. 5 (Sept.–Oct. 1998).]

10 [For a brilliant analysis of the "Constantinianizing" of the church and its effects, see the following by John Howard Yoder: "The Disavowal of Constantine," *The Royal Priesthood: Essays Ecclesiological and Ecumenical,* ed. Michael Cartwright (Grand Rapids, Mich.: Eerdmans, 1994); and "The Constantinian Sources of Western Social Ethics," *The Priestly Kingdom: Social Ethics as Gospel* (Notre Dame, Ind.: University of Notre Dame Press, 1984).]

[11] [For a concise survey of these movements, see Eberhard Arnold, *The Early Anabaptists* (Farmington, Pa.: Plough, 1984).]

[12] [On the relevance of Jubilee norms for society in general, see Michael Schluter and Roy Clements, "Jubilee Institutional Norms: A Middle Way between Creation Ethics and Kingdom Ethics as the Basis for Christian Political Action," *Evangelical Quarterly* 62, no.1 (1990), pp. 37–62.]

Chapter 6: Precursors to Peace

[1] Later Jesus would say, "...Be sons of your Father in heaven. He causes his sun to rise on the evil and the good, and sends rain on the righteous and the unrighteous" (Matt. 5:45).

[2] Cf. the end of chapter 1. ["It is in this way that he triumphs over sin, guilt, and death. It involves a double coincidence. Evil culminates in murder; by *taking away* the life of the other person, sin brings about the successful conclusion of its essential intention, the rejection of the Lord and of whoever bears his image. By contrast, love, which is 'being for the other person,' culminates in the *gift* of one's own life in favor of someone else." Henri Blocher, *Evil and the Cross* (Downers Grove, Ill.: InterVarsity Press, 1994), p. 132.]

[3] [For an excellent treatment of this period, see Stephen F. Noll, *The Intertestamental Period: A Study Guide* (Madison, Wis.: InterVarsity Press, 1985). See also Richard Horsley, *Galilee: History, Politics, People* (Valley Forge, Pa.: Trinity Press International, 1995).]

[4] Several times in history, great religious movements, beginning with a fervent preoccupation with being strictly faithful to God, have degenerated into violence and civil war. Muhammad, who had been forced to flee from Mecca in 622, gave up his earlier patience and began to attack the caravans of his enemies. Luther in 1525, fearing the excesses of the revolting peasants, abandoned nonviolence and advised the princes to use violence against them. He also ordered believers to support the princes. In France, Gaspard de Coligny, shocked by the news of the Vassy massacre of 1562 and tired of seeing his defenseless fellow believers imprisoned, tortured, and assassinated, decided to take up arms and thus opened the era of religious wars. Jesus, on the other hand, always refused to be drawn into armed resistance. The early Christians followed their master's example, though few Christian groups do so today.

Chapter 7: Crises in Palestine

[1] Jesus' parable of the ten minas, discussed in chapter 4, probably refers to this historical event.

² Josephus, *Jewish Antiquities*, XVIII, V, 2.

³ ["The causes of this unrest were many and varied, but the following factors contributed to a milieu ripe for revolution: foreign military occupation, class conflicts, misconduct of Jewish and Roman officials, Hellenization, burdensome taxation and the Samaritan situation. When the Roman army occupied a land, it was accompanied by thousands of civilians (wives, children, doctors, merchants, etc.). The army lived off the occupied country, pilfering its natural resources, enslaving members of its population, raping women and generally terrorizing the populace. The gentry of Palestine collaborated with the occupying forces and, in exchange for personal safety and affluence, aided Israel's oppressors. This collusion led to class conflict between the rich and the poor, the faithful and the unfaithful, the rulers and the people." W. J. Heard, "Revolutionary Movements," in *Dictionary of Jesus and the Gospels,* eds. Joel B. Green, Scot McKnight (Downers Grove, Ill.: InterVarsity Press, 1992), p. 688.]

⁴ [Experts would now place the percentage lower. But by any measure, the burden on small landowners was extraordinary. "In addition to his need to save for the sabbatical year, the double system demanded from 35 to 40 percent of his produce, perhaps even more." Borg, *Conflict, Holiness, and Politics in the Teachings of Jesus,* p. 48.]

⁵ We have seen how a creditor could have his insolvent debtor sold, along with his wife, children, and possessions. In the parable of the unforgiving servant, Jesus tells about one of these sales, which he may have seen with his own eyes.

Chapter 8: Resistance Movements

¹ [This is yet another indication that certain jubilean practices were observed.] Some historians have questioned the authenticity of this edict, whose complete text is recorded by Josephus along with some local decrees concerning its application. These historians point out that Jews could be found in the armies of Herod and surrounding kings. No doubt some impious Jews did enroll voluntarily in these armies, but it is clear that no faithful Jew could perform military service either in the Roman legions or in the auxiliary troops because of his religious beliefs and practices.

² Josephus, *Jewish Antiquities,* XVIII, III, 5.

³ Ibid., XVIII, I, I.

⁴ Josephus, *Jewish Wars,* I, XXXIII, 2–4.

⁵ Ibid., I, XXXIII, 6.

⁶ Ibid., II, I, 1–3.

7 [Trocmé's description of the Zealots needs to be modified at this point. The Zealot party per se was not formed until the winter of A.D. 67–68. Moreover, although other resistance groups could be called "zealots" because of their similar ideology, more recent scholarship clearly distinguishes various armed resistance groups – social bandits, *Sicarii*, Zealots, messianic pretenders, revolutionary prophets, the Fourth Philosophy. See Heard, "Revolutionary Movements," *Dictionary of Jesus and the Gospels*, pp. 688–698; Stegemann and Stegemann, *The Jesus Movement*, pp. 171–172; and Borg, *Conflict, Holiness, and Politics in the Teachings of Jesus*, ch. 2.]

8 Josephus, *Jewish Antiquities*, XVIII, I, 6. The Gospels recount how some of Jesus' listeners tried to trap him and make him say that one should refuse to pay tribute to Caesar. By agreeing with them, Jesus would have sided with the Zealots. Did he not say, as they did, that we should have no master but God? (Matt. 23:8–10).

9 Josephus, *Jewish Antiquities*, XVII, X, 6–8. Josephus summarizes the situation: "And so Judea was filled with brigandage. Anyone might make himself king as the head of a band of rebels whom he fell in with, and then would press on to the destruction of the community, causing trouble to few Romans and then only to a small degree but bringing the greatest slaughter upon their own people."

10 Acts 5:33–41. See also Josephus, *Jewish Antiquities*, XX, V, 1–2.

11 [Paul was accused in Philippi of "throwing our city into an uproar by advocating customs unlawful for us Romans to accept or practice," and in Jerusalem of being "the man who teaches all men everywhere against our people and our law and this place" (Acts 16:20–21; 21:28). And in Thessalonica he was also accused of being one of those "who have caused trouble all over the world" (Acts 17:6). Bruce explains the gravity of the charge: "Jason and his friends were charged with harboring Jewish agitators, political messianists such as had stirred up unrest in other cities of the Roman Empire…Their seditious and revolutionary activity was not only illegal in itself; they were actually proclaiming one, Jesus, as a rival emperor to him who ruled in Rome." F. F. Bruce, *The Book of Acts*, New International Commentary on the New Testament, rev. ed. (Grand Rapids, Mich.: Eerdmans, 1988), pp. 324–325. See also James D. G. Dunn, "Caesar, Consul, Governor," *The New International Dictionary of New Testament Theology*, Colin Brown, ed., vol. I (Grand Rapids, Mich.: Zondervan, 1986). For a thorough treatment of the social and political elements in Acts, see Richard J. Cassidy, *Society and Politics in the Acts of the Apostles* (Maryknoll, N.Y.: Orbis, 1987).]

12 Josephus, *Jewish Wars*, II, XIII, 3. See also Josephus, *Jewish Antiquities*, XX, VIII, 5.

13 Ibid., II, XIII, 4–5.

Chapter 9: Seeds of Nonviolence

1 Josephus, *Jewish Wars,* II, IX, 2–3.

2 Josephus, *Jewish Wars,* II, IX, 4; *Jewish Antiquities,* XVIII, III, 2.

3 Josephus, *Jewish Antiquities,* XVIII, VIII.

4 [Yoder identifies four ways: conservative realism, revolutionary violence, withdrawal, and "proper religion." He also notes that in contradistinction to these four options, Jesus came to create a distinct community "with its own deviant set of values" and its own coherent way of incarnating them – "a society like no other society." John Howard Yoder, *The Original Revolution* (Scottdale, Pa.: Herald Press, 1977), pp. 18–33.]

5 [See Cassidy, *Jesus, Politics, and Society,* pp. 121–123.]

6 There was something tragic about the conflict between Jesus and the Pharisees, because Jesus' faith generally corresponded with the Pharisees' piety. Both had fervent confidence in God, an expectation of messianic times, and hope in the resurrection of the dead. Had the Pharisees been moved by Jesus' appeal, history would have been different. Unfortunately, they took the lead in rejecting and condemning him. See Chapter 12.

7 The Dead Sea Scrolls describe a "wicked high priest" who persecuted the "Teacher of Righteousness," perhaps the founder of the Essene order, "in order to confuse him by a display of violent temper, desiring to exile him,…[and who] wrought abominable works…defiled the sanctuary of God…plundered the property of the needy." Some historians have stressed the resemblance between the "Teacher of Righteousness" and Jesus. However, the manuscripts do not give the death of the Teacher of Righteousness a redemptive character.

8 [For instance, Jesus' directive in Matthew 18:15–20. This instruction is a restatement of Leviticus 19:17–18. The Essenes also emphasized the importance of mutual rebuke and correction, citing Leviticus 19 as the scriptural basis for this practice. See *Community Rule,* 5.25–6.1; *Damascus Document,* 9.2–4.]

9 [Scholars disagree about how Jesus related to these various groups, sometimes assuming that he must have belonged to one. However, the Gospels fail to relate Jesus to any specific group. He was simply a devout Jewish layman. (See Meier, *A Marginal Jew,* vol. 1, pp. 345–49.) Put differently, Jesus' relationship with the various movements of his day was one of critical juxtaposition. "Jesus connected, in many ways, with each of the major Jewish sects of the day. And yet, he also differed with them…Against *all* the major Jewish sects, Jesus focused far more on morality than on ritual, announced the arrival of the

kingdom, stressed love for all peoples, even one's enemies, and claimed that he was the Messiah who was one with God." Blomberg, *Jesus and the Gospels*, p. 398.]

[10] ["What the whole history of Jesus shows is not the apolitical character of the kingdom he proclaims, nor pure pacifism – understood as an absence of struggle – as the way to build it, but a different understanding of how to do it. The kingdom he glimpses does not mean getting back into power, and so Jesus did not share the heady religious nationalisms or the theories of political theocracy upheld by the Zealots. This kingdom, in contrast, was to be expressed and established by the best of human values: by the power of truth, justice and love. It was to be established – and this is the greatest difference from all other groups – by grace." Jon Sobrino, *Jesus the Liberator: A Historical-Theological View* (Maryknoll, N.Y.: Orbis, 1993), p. 215.]

Chapter 10: Another Way

[1] ["We understand Jesus only if we can empathize with this threefold rejection: the self-evident, axiomatic, sweeping rejection of both quietism and establishment responsibility, and the difficult, constantly reopened, genuinely attractive option of the crusade." Yoder, *The Politics of Jesus*, p. 97.]

[2] [Trocmé's use of the term "Zealots" should be understood as a designation to identify collectively all groups that engaged in violent resistance. See note 7, ch. 8.]

[3] The word "Iscariot" may be a deformation of the word *sicarii*, the Latin equivalent of "zealot." Traditionally, "Iscariot" has been said to mean "man of Karioth" *(ish-Karioth),* a citizen of Karioth. [For a discussion addressing whether Jesus was a Zealot, see Oscar Cullmann, *Jesus and the Revolutionaries* (New York: Harper & Row, 1970).]

[4] Revolutionaries often have to fight on two fronts: against the enemies of their people and against reactionaries who oppose revolution. In Jesus' mind the latter came first because he believed, with the prophets, that God would liberate his people as soon as they would obey his voice.

[5] [For a more detailed analysis on the temptation of violence, see Yoder, *The Politics of Jesus*, ch. 2.]

[6] Many of today's conscientious objectors are criticized for being "out of touch with reality." "If you want to break with the world," they are told, "go live on a desert island." But their nonviolent stand is precisely for the sake of this world. Christ's kingdom must be present in the world like leaven in bread.

7   Luther developed this notion known as the "doctrine of the two kingdoms." [For a critique of this view from within the Lutheran persuasion, see Dietrich Bonhoeffer, *The Cost of Discipleship* (New York: Macmillan, 1958), pp. 120–133.]

8   This passage brings to mind the scene where Jesus looked upon all the kingdoms of this world, but refused to conquer them by the means the tempter proposed (Luke 4:5–8).

9   We have already mentioned the collusion between the Sanhedrin and the Romans at the time of Jesus' trial. If Jesus had chosen violence, he would have set off both a war of national liberation and a civil war.

Chapter 11: The Radical Explosion

1   Josephus, *Jewish Antiquities,* XVIII, II, 2.

2   Josephus, *Jewish Wars,* II, XII, 3–6; *Jewish Antiquities,* XX, VI, 1–3.

3   This pithy remark and the decision to go elsewhere define exactly, both theologically and pragmatically, what Christian nonviolence is.

4   [Jesus lived in a culture in which men usually viewed women in negative terms. Women were limited to domestic roles, and were thought to be responsible for most sin, especially sexual temptation and immorality. Typical is the view expressed in Sirach: "Better is the wickedness of a man than a woman who does good; it is woman who brings shame and disgrace" (Sir. 42:14). And according to the rabbinic Tosefta, a Jewish man prayed three benedictions each day, including one in which he thanked God that he was not made a woman (t. Ber. 7:18).]

5   [All four Gospels attest to the fact that a group of women followed (*akaloutheo,* as "disciples") Jesus in Galilee and to Jerusalem, where they were present at his crucifixion, burial, and resurrection (Matt. 27:55–28:1; Mark 15:40–16:1; Luke 8:1–3, 23:49–24:1; John 19:25–27, 20:1).]

6   Cf. Matt. 8:21–22, 12:46–50, 19:29; Luke 9:57–62, 12:49–53.

7   [For a comprehensive and balanced survey of Jesus' understanding of women, see B. Witherington III, *Women in the Ministry of Jesus: A Study of Jesus' Attitudes to Women and Their Roles* (Cambridge: Cambridge University Press, 1984).]

Chapter 12: The Sword of the Spirit

1   Later called the Talmud and the Mishnah.

2   "They are extremely influential among the people, and all divine worship, prayers, and sacrifices are performed according to their direction. The cities give great attestations to them on account of their virtuous conduct, both in the actions of their lives and in their discourses." Josephus, *Jewish Antiquities,* XVIII, I, 3.

3   [Jesus re-conceives "holiness" in terms of human need. His reference point was the human condition, not code—be it defined religiously, morally, socially, or otherwise.]

4   Cf. Matt. 9:16–17; Luke 5:36–39.

Chapter 13: Nonviolent Love and the Person

1   The most explicit passage is found in John 6: "I am the living bread that came down from heaven. If anyone eats of this bread, he will live forever. This bread is my flesh, which I will give for the life of the world" (v. 51). [Trocmé may be overstating his point here as there seem to be several theological indicators in the Gospels that point to redemptive suffering. See John R.W. Stott, *The Cross of Christ* (Downers Grove, Ill.: InterVarsity, 1986).]

2   Cf. Matt. 12:1–14; Mark 2:23 3:6.

3   [For example, the issue of "collateral damage" in time of war.]

4   Today, either to liberate the world from the exploitation of capitalism or the danger of communism [or to free it from imperialism or terrorism], people on both sides justify the use of force, even if the moral categories of innocent and guilty break down.

5   [One could safely add World War II to this list.]

6   Exod. 31:14–15. The Mishnah adds, "They may not set a broken limb. If a man's hand or foot is dislocated he may not pour cold water over it, but he may wash it after his usual fashion and if he is healed in this way, he is healed" (Mishnah, Sabbath XXII, 6).

7   The unfaithfulness of some Christians becomes obvious in view of their priorities. They think economic and political necessities cannot wait, whereas God has plenty of time. But in Jesus' eyes, God cannot wait! Economic and political matters, whose importance he does not underestimate, will be better served if God comes first.

8   "Bundles of straw, bundles of branches, and bundles of young shoots may be removed from their place if they were put in readiness before the Sabbath as cattle fodder, if not they may not be removed" (Mishnah, Sabbath XVIII, 2).

⁹ The false dilemma can be stated as follows: to use violence or to allow the wicked to do as he pleases; to use the sword or to be a coward.

¹⁰ Jesus never advocated the tyrannical heroism of group solidarity. Peter thought he could "give his life" with Jesus: "Lord, why can't I follow you now? I will lay down my life for you." But Jesus put him back in his place: "Will you really lay down your life for me? I tell you the truth, before the rooster crows, you will disown me three times!" (John 13:37).

¹¹ Luke 23:28, 22:51, 23:43, 23:34 respectively.

Chapter 14: The Greatest Commandment

¹ [Some of Jesus' strongest words are aimed at hypocrites. See Matt. 6:2–5, 7:5, 15:7–9, 22:15–18, 23:3–5, 13ff.; Luke 6:42, 12:54–56, 13:15.]

² [On the imperative of practicing the *whole* gospel to the *whole* person, see Ronald J. Sider, *Good News and Good Works: A Theology of the Whole Gospel* (Grand Rapids, Mich.: Baker Books, 1993).]

³ [This point is amplified and developed by Eberhard Arnold, *God's Revolution: Justice, Community, and the Coming Kingdom* (Farmington, Pa.: Plough, 1997), pp. 157–168.]

⁴ [On the theme of violence begetting more violence, see Jacques Ellul, *Violence: Reflections from a Christian Perspective* (New York: Seabury Press, 1969).]

⁵ [Nonviolence presupposes "possibility" over against the "necessity" of using force. In every situation, there is a moral and pragmatic alternative to violence. See John Howard Yoder, *What Would You Do?* (Scottdale, Pa.: Herald Press, 1983). On the theme of God's new possibility, see Isa. 43:18,19; Luke 18:26,27; Rom. 7:4–6; 1 Cor. 10:11–13; 2 Cor. 5:17; Eph. 2:11–18; Phil. 4:11–13; Rev. 3:8.]

⁶ [Trocmé asserts that justice is crucial to Jesus' message. He is against the dualism that separates Jesus from matters related to the state. Yoder too, in *For the Nations*, argues that the church should speak to the state directly because Christ is lord over all, not only over the church. This differentiates Trocmé and Yoder from Hauerwas, who consistently argues that only by embodying a social ethic–only by *being* signposts of God's peaceable kingdom–can we help the world, and the state, see what it is not, and thereby serve as an agent of its healing. See the following works by Stanley Hauerwas: *The Peaceable Kingdom* (Notre Dame, Ind.: University of Notre Dame Press, 1983), ch. 6; *Against the Nations* (Minneapolis: Winston Press, 1985), chs. 2–3, 6–7; *Christian Existence Today* (Durham, N.C.: Labyrinth Press, 1988); *Resident Aliens*

(Nashville: Abingdon Press, 1989); *After Christendom?* (Nashville: Abingdon Press, 1991), chs. 2 & 6.]

7   The Greek text uses the verb *antistenai,* which means "to face someone for a fight," and should be translated: "Do not fight evil with the same weapons." [For an extended discussion on *antistenai* and the implications of this passage, see Walter Wink, *The Powers That Be* (New York: Doubleday, 1998), ch. 5. On the general theme of loving the enemy from within a biblical framework, see William Klassen, *Love of Enemies: The Way to Peace* (Philadelphia: Fortress, 1984).]

8   For Gandhi, nonviolence was also more than a means toward an end. It was also a witness to God, but Gandhi placed his spirituality in the service of an immediate political end. This Jesus did not do.

9   *Young India* (Oct. 8, 1925), p. 346.

10 [The success of nonviolence is often ignored. On the pragmatics of nonviolence as well as its relevance to national and international conflict, see G. Simon Harak, S.J., ed., *Nonviolence for the Third Millennium* (Macon, Ga.: Mercer University Press, 2000); Michael Henderson, *The Forgiveness Factor: Stories of Hope in a World of Conflict* (London: Grosvenor Books, 1996); Donald W. Shriver, Jr., *An Ethic for Enemies* (New York: Oxford University Press, 1995); Glen Stassen, ed., *Just Peacemaking: Ten Practices for Abolishing War* (Cleveland: Pilgrim Press, 1998).]

11 Gandhi called his disciples to what he termed "voluntary suffering": absolute truth, chastity, poverty, and no possessions.

12 [See Matt. 6:13, 12:28; John 12:31, 16:11, 17:15.]

13 [See 2 Pet. 3:9,15; 1 Tim. 2:4; 2 Cor. 5:17–19.]

14 *Young India* (Dec. 31, 1931), p. 427.

15 [See Peter Ackerman and Jack Duval, *A Force More Powerful: A Century of Nonviolent Conflict* (New York: Palgrave, 2000); and Staughton Lynd and Alice Lynd, eds., *Nonviolence in America: A Documentary History* (Maryknoll, N.Y.: Orbis, 1995).]

16 [Bonhoeffer refers to this as "cheap grace." See Bonhoeffer, *The Cost of Discipleship,* ch. 1.]

17 [See Eph. 2:4–10. Hays points out: "The sense of imminence of the coming of the Lord heightens rather than negates the imperatives of ethical action. The community is called to pursue with urgency the tasks of love and mutual service." Hays, *The Moral Vision of the New Testament,* p. 26.]

Chapter 15: The Politics of Witness

1   See Matt. 13. [For a classic discussion of the church's relationship to the world, see H. Richard Niebuhr, *Christ and Culture* (New York: Harper, 1951). For an incisive critique of Niebuhr, see Glen H. Stassen, D.M. Yeager, and John Howard Yoder, *Authentic Transformation: A New Vision of Christ and Culture* (Nashville: Abingdon Press, 1998). Other works of relevance are Robert E. Webber, *The Church in the World: Opposition, Tension, or Transformation* (Grand Rapids, Mich.: Zondervan, 1986); Charles Scriven, *The Transformation of Culture* (Scottdale, Pa.: Herald Press, 1988); C. Norman Kraus, *The Authentic Witness* (Scottdale, Pa.: Herald Press, 1979), ch. 7; Eberhard Arnold, *Salt and Light: Living the Sermon on the Mount* (Farmington, Pa.: Plough, 1967).]

2   [The following address the relative nature of the state and are sympathetic to Trocmé's approach: Hendrik Berkhof, *Christ and the Powers* (Scottdale, Pa.: Herald Press, 1977); John Howard Yoder, *The Christian Witness to the State* (Newton, Kans.: Faith and Life Press, 1964); Vernard Eller, *Christian Anarchy* (Grand Rapids, Mich.: Eerdmans, 1987).]

3   [For a hard-hitting discussion on the problem of morally justifying war, see John Howard Yoder, *When War is Unjust* (Minneapolis, Minn.: Augsburg Press, 1984). On the so-called justifiability of specific U.S. military actions, see William Blum, *Killing Hope: U.S. Military and CIA Intervention Since WWII* (Monroe, Maine: Common Courage Press, 1995).]

4   Cf. John 8:12, 9:5; Luke 12:35.

5   [Father George Zabelka, chaplain for the Hiroshima and Nagasaki bomb squads, recounts the church's complicity in the bombing of civilians: "To fail to speak to the utter moral corruption of the mass destruction of civilians was to fail as a Christian and as a priest…I was there, and I'll tell you that the operational moral atmosphere in the church in relation to mass bombing of enemy civilians was totally indifferent, silent, and corrupt at best—at worst it was religiously supportive of these activities by blessing those who did them…Catholics dropped the A-bomb on top of the largest and first Catholic city in Japan…One would have thought that I would have suggested that, as a minimal standard of Catholic morality, Catholics shouldn't bomb Catholic children. I didn't. I, like the Catholic pilot of the Nagasaki plane, 'The Great Artiste,' was heir to a Christianity that had for seventeen hundred years engaged in revenge, murder, torture, the pursuit of power, and prerogative violence, all in the name of our Lord." George Zabelka, "I Was Told It Was Necessary," *Sojourners* (Sept. 8, 1980), pp. 12–15.]

Chapter 16: God's History

[1] [Yoder argues similarly in *The Christian Witness to the State*.]

[2] See Eph. 2:11–22; 1 Pet. 3:8–18.

[3] [The counterintuitive paradoxes of the Beatitudes alone point to the fact that
Jesus' new way gives birth to a contrast society (Gerhard Lohfink), out of
synch with the "normal" order of the world. The kingdom of God turns the
world upside down (Donald Kraybill) not through armed revolution but
through the formation of a new society (John Stott), a counterintuitive culture
(Rodney Clapp), an alternative witness-bearing community (John Howard
Yoder). For a general discussion regarding "reversal," see Donald Kraybill, *The
Upside-Down Kingdom* (Scottdale, Pa.: Herald Press, 1978). On the church as
a "contrast society," see Gerhard Lohfink, *Jesus and Community* (Philadelphia:
Fortress, 1984).]

[4] [By "program" Trocmé does not mean a political "platform." He is referring
more to what Rodney Clapp calls "depth politics," meaning any "deliberate
and structured attempt to influence how people live in society." The church
is a "depth-political community." Rodney Clapp, *People of the Truth* (Harrisburg, Pa.: Morehouse Publishing, 1993), pp. 12, 52.]

[5] [In the first edition, Trocmé argued, among other things, that due to the tardi-
ness of Jesus' return, second-generation Christians shifted their understanding
away from an earthly kingdom to a spiritual one. This could be. The general
consensus on what Jesus meant regarding the "imminence" of the kingdom,
however, ties it closely to the "last days," which refers *both* to the eschatological age of the Spirit and to the end of that age. Hays puts it well: "The
church community is God's eschatological beachhead, the place where the
power of God has invaded the world…What is God doing in the world in
the interval between resurrection and *parousia*? According to Paul, God is at
work through the Spirit to create communities that prefigure and embody the
reconciliation and healing of the world." Hays, *The Moral Vision of the New
Testament*, pp. 27, 32.]

[6] [Put differently, Martin Luther King notes, "Means and ends must cohere
because the end is preexistent in the means, and ultimately destructive means
cannot bring about constructive ends…The means we use must be as pure
as the ends we seek." Alex Ayres, ed., *The Wisdom of Martin Luther King, Jr.*
(New York: Meridan, 1993), pp. 150–151.]

[7] [Commenting on the Sermon on the Mount, Hays concludes: "Matthew offers
a vision of a radical counter-cultural community of discipleship characterized
by a "higher righteousness"–a community free of anger, lust, falsehood, and

violence. The transcendence of violence through loving the enemy is the most salient feature of this new model *polis*..." Hays, *The Moral Vision of the New Testament*, p. 322.]

8   [A reference to Luther. For an excellent summary, see Robert E. Webber, *The Church in the World*, ch. 8.]

9   The Nuremberg trials and atrocities committed by Christian nations in Algeria and Vietnam have also underlined the absurdity of blind obedience to orders.

10 Rapid progress in medicine is shrinking the area of life where the church still has some usefulness.

11 [Post-critical thought confirms Trocmé on this point. "Myth" in this sense has less to do with fanciful or wishful thinking and more to do with making sense of our worlds. Crossan notes how "myth establishes world" (p. 59). Hauerwas argues that "Our metaphors and stories entice us to find a way to bring into existence the reality that at once should be, but will not be, except as we act as if it is" (p. 73). The work of Eliade, Ricoeur, Wilder, and others demonstrate the connection between myth and experience. See John Dominic Crossan, *The Dark Interval: Towards a Theology of Story* (Niles, Ill.: Argus Communications, 1975); Stanley Hauerwas, *Vision and Virtue* (Notre Dame, Ind.: University of Notre Dame Press, 1974); Mircea Eliade, *Myth and Reality* (New York: Harper & Row, 1963); Amos Wilder, "Story and Story World" in *Interpretation*, 37, no. 4 (Oct. 1983); George Lakoff and Mark Johnson, *Metaphors We Live By* (Chicago: University of Chicago Press, 1983).]

Select Bibliography

Ackerman, Peter, and Jack Duval. *A Force More Powerful: A Century of Nonviolent Conflict.* New York: Palgrave, 2000.

Beasley-Murray, G. R. *Jesus and the Kingdom of God.* Grand Rapids, Mich.: Eerdmans, 1986.

Blomberg, Craig L. *Jesus and the Gospels.* Nashville: Broadman & Holman, 1997.

Borg, Marcus J. *Conflict, Holiness, and Politics in the Teachings of Jesus.* Harrisburg, Pa.: Trinity Press International, 1998.

Cassidy, Richard J. *Jesus, Politics, and Society: A Study of Luke's Gospel.* Maryknoll, N.Y.: Orbis, 1978.

Crossan, John Dominic. *The Birth of Christianity.* New York: Harper San Francisco, 1998.

Cullmann, Oscar. *Jesus and the Revolutionaries.* New York: Harper & Row, 1970.

Fuellenbach, John. *The Kingdom of God: The Message of Jesus Today.* Maryknoll, N.Y.: Orbis, 1995.

Gnuse, Robert. *You Shall Not Steal: Community and Property in the Biblical Tradition.* Maryknoll, N.Y.: Orbis, 1985.

Hauerwas, Stanley. *After Christendom?* Nashville: Abingdon Press, 1991.

———. *Against the Nations.* Minneapolis: Winston Press, 1985.

———. *Christian Existence Today.* Durham, N.C.: Labyrinth Press, 1988.

———. *The Peaceable Kingdom.* Notre Dame, Ind.: University of Notre Dame Press, 1983.

———. *Resident Aliens.* Nashville: Abingdon Press, 1989.

Hays, Richard B. *The Moral Vision of the New Testament: A Contemporary Introduction to New Testament Ethics.* New York: Harper San Francisco, 1996.

Heard, W. J. "Revolutionary Moments." In *Dictionary of Jesus and the Gospels.* Edited by Joel B. Green and Scot McKnight. Downers Grove, Ill.: InterVarsity Press, 1992.

Horsley, Richard. *Galilee: History, Politics, People.* Valley Forge, Pa.: Trinity Press International, 1995.

Kraybill, Donald. *The Upside-Down Kingdom.* Scottdale, Pa.: Herald Press, 1978.

Lohfink, Gerhard. *Jesus and Community.* Philadelphia: Fortress, 1984.

Lowery, Richard H. *Sabbath and Jubilee.* St. Louis, Mo.: Chalice Press, 2000.

Meier, John P. *A Marginal Jew: Rethinking the Historical Jesus.* 3 vols. New York: Doubleday, 1991–1994; New York: Anchor, 2001.

Myers, Ched. *Who Will Roll Away the Stone? Discipleship Queries for First World Christians.* Maryknoll, N.Y.: Orbis, 1995.

North, Robert. *Sociology of the Biblical Jubilee.* Analecta Biblica, no. 4. Rome: Pontifical Biblical Institute, 1954.

Pixley, George V. *God's Kingdom: A Guide for Biblical Study.* Maryknoll, N.Y.: Orbis, 1981.

Ringe, Sharon. *Jesus, Liberation, and Biblical Jubilee.* Philadelphia: Fortress, 1985.

Sanders, E. P. *Jesus and Judaism.* Philadelphia: Fortress, 1985.

Sauvage, Pierre, dir. *Weapons of the Spirit.* Los Angeles: Chambon Foundation, 1989. Documentary film.

Sobrino, Jon. *Jesus the Liberator: A Historical-Theological View.* Maryknoll, N.Y.: Orbis, 1993.

Stegemann, Ekkehard W. and Wolfgang Stegemann. *The Jesus Movement: A Social History of Its First Century.* Minneapolis: Fortress, 1999.

Webber, Robert E. *The Church in the World: Opposition, Tension, or Transformation.* Grand Rapids, Mich.: Zondervan, 1986.

Wink, Walter. *The Powers That Be.* New York: Doubleday, 1998.

Wright, N. T. *The Challenge of Jesus: Rediscovering Who Jesus Was and Is.* Downers Grove, Ill.: InterVarsity, 1999.

———. *Jesus and the Victory of God.* Minneapolis: Fortress, 1996.

Yoder, John Howard. *The Christian Witness to the State.* Newton, Kans.: Faith and Life Press, 1964.

———. *The Politics of Jesus,* 2nd ed. Grand Rapids, Mich.: Eerdmans, 1994.

———. *The Priestly Kingdom: Social Ethics as Gospel.* Notre Dame, Ind.: University of Notre Dame Press, 1984.

————. *The Royal Priesthood: Essays Ecclesiological and Ecumenical.* Edited by Michael Cartwright. Grand Rapids, Mich.: Eerdmans, 1994.

————. *What Would You Do?* Scottdale, Pa.: Herald Press, 1983.

Scripture Index

Old Testament

New Testament

Index